Honour-Based Abuse

Editor: Danielle Lobban

Volume 443

independence
educational publishers

First published by Independence Educational Publishers

The Studio, High Green

Great Shelford

Cambridge CB22 5EG

England

© Independence 2024

ISBN-13: 978 1 86168 903 0

Printed in Great Britain

Zenith Print Group

Acknowledgements

The publisher is grateful for permission to reproduce the material in this book. While every care has been taken to trace and acknowledge copyright, the publisher tenders its apology for any accidental infringement or where copyright has proved untraceable. The publisher would be pleased to come to a suitable arrangement in any such case with the rightful owner.

The material reproduced in **issues** books is provided as an educational resource only. The views, opinions and information contained within reprinted material in **issues** books do not necessarily represent those of Independence Educational Publishers and its employees.

Images

Cover image courtesy of iStock. All other images courtesy of Freepik, Pixabay and Unsplash, except page 10: Janey Hills

Additional acknowledgements

With thanks to the Independence team: Janey Hills, Klaudia Sommer and Jackie Staines.

Danielle Lobban

Cambridge, May 2024

Contents

Introduction

Honour-Based Abuse is volume 443 in the **issues** series. The aim of the series is to offer current, diverse information about important issues in our world, from a UK perspective.

About *Honour Based Abuse*

The true number of victims of so-called honour based abuse is unknown as many women and girls are suffering in silence. At least one 'honour' killing a month happens in the UK. This book looks at the many different types of abuse and explores the reasons behind the abuse.

Our sources

Titles in the **issues** series are designed to function as educational resource books, providing a balanced overview of a specific subject.

The information in our books is comprised of facts, articles and opinions from many different sources, including:

- Newspaper reports and opinion pieces
- Website factsheets
- Magazine and journal articles
- Statistics and surveys
- Government reports
- Literature from special interest groups.

A note on critical evaluation

Because the information reprinted here is from a number of different sources, readers should bear in mind the origin of the text and whether the source is likely to have a particular bias when presenting information (or when conducting their research). It is hoped that, as you read about the many aspects of the issues explored in this book, you will critically evaluate the information presented.

It is important that you decide whether you are being presented with facts or opinions. Does the writer give a biased or unbiased report? If an opinion is being expressed, do you agree with the writer? Is there potential bias to the 'facts' or statistics behind an article?

Activities

Throughout this book, you will find a selection of assignments and activities designed to help you engage with the articles you have been reading and to explore your own opinions. Some tasks will take longer than others and there is a mixture of design, writing and research-based activities that you can complete alone or in a group.

Further research

At the end of each article we have listed its source and a website that you can visit if you would like to conduct your own research. Please remember to critically evaluate any sources that you consult and consider whether the information you are viewing is accurate and unbiased.

Issues Online

The **issues** series of books is complemented by our online resource, issuesonline.co.uk

On the Issues Online website you will find a wealth of information, covering over 70 topics, to support the PSHE and RSE curriculum.

Why Issues Online?

Researching a topic? Issues Online is the best place to start for...

Librarians

Issues Online is an essential tool for librarians: feel confident you are signposting safe, reliable, user-friendly online resources to students and teaching staff alike. We provide multi-user concurrent access, so no waiting around for another student to finish with a resource. Issues Online also provides FREE downloadable posters for your shelf/wall/table displays.

Teachers

Issues Online is an ideal resource for lesson planning, inspiring lively debate in class and setting lessons and homework tasks.

Our accessible, engaging content helps deepen students' knowledge, promotes critical thinking and develops independent learning skills.

Issues Online saves precious preparation time. We wade through the wealth of material on the internet to filter the best quality, most relevant and up-to-date information you need to start exploring a topic.

Our carefully selected, balanced content presents an overview and insight into each topic from a variety of sources and viewpoints.

Students

Issues Online is designed to support your studies in a broad range of topics, particularly social issues relevant to young people today.

There are thousands of articles, statistics and infographs instantly available to help you with research and assignments.

With 24/7 access using the powerful Algolia search system, you can find relevant information quickly, easily and safely anytime from your laptop, tablet or smartphone, in class or at home.

Visit issuesonline.co.uk to find out more!

issues online
resources for schools, colleges & libraries

What is Honour Based Abuse?

Honour Based Abuse is widely misunderstood, meaning that hundreds of victims are not being helped and perpetrators are escaping justice.

Honour based abuse can take many forms, including child marriage, virginity testing, enforced abortion, forced marriage, female genital mutilation, as well as physical, sexual and economic abuse and coercive control.

There is currently little accurate data on the true extent of Honour based abuse and its impact on women and girls – its true scale, scope and prevalence is not known, and so it remains a thriving but invisible problem.

A form of domestic abuse

Honour Based Abuse is often thought of as a 'cultural', 'traditional' or 'religious' problem. It can affect people of all ages, but often begins early in the family home.

It can lead to a deeply embedded form of coercive control, built on expectations about acceptable and unacceptable behaviours. Control is often established without overt violence against the victim. For example, family members may threaten to kill themselves or ostracise the victim.

Perpetrators are often partners or ex-partners, or family members. We know, through calls to our national Honour Based Abuse Helpline, that most victims experience abuse from multiple perpetrators, including parents and siblings.

Facts and figures

- Victims of honour based abuse experience abuse for much longer than those not identified as at risk of Honour Based Abuse

- Victims of honour based abuse are seven times more likely to experience abuse from multiple perpetrators, and are at greater risk of serious harm or homicide

- Research suggests that at least one 'honour' killing occurs in the UK every month (and this is likely to be an underestimate)

> My husband would beat me daily. I desperately wanted to leave, but my parents and in-laws encouraged me to make it work. They would say to me: What will people say? The fear of bringing shame and the lack of family support trapped me in that marriage for 14 years.
>
> – Kal, Helpline caller

- Karma Nirvana support over 2,000 victims of honour based abuse every year

The concept of 'honour'

For some communities, the concept of 'honour' is prized above the safety and wellbeing of individuals. To compromise a family's 'honour' is to bring dishonour and shame – which can have severe consequences.

This is sometimes used to justify emotional abuse, physical abuse, disownment and in some cases even murder.

Definitions

There is currently no statutory definition of honour based abuse in England and Wales, but a common definition has been adopted across government and criminal justice agencies: 'A crime or incident which has, or may have been, committed to protect or defend the honour of the family and/or community'.

Which communities are affected?

Honour based abuse is more prevalent within communities from South Asia, the Middle East, and North and East Africa. Reports come from Muslim, Sikh, Hindu, Orthodox Jewish and occasionally traveller communities. It is not determined by gender – both perpetrators and victims can be male or female.

However, cultural tradition does not mean honour based abuse is acceptable. Forced marriage is illegal. All forms of domestic abuse are illegal.

www.karmanirvana.org.uk

'Honour-based' violence

You may have been told you have brought 'shame' on your family or community, or given them a 'bad name.' When someone in your family or community hurts or threatens to hurt you because of this, it is called 'honour-based' violence (HBV).

Many young people experiencing HBV think it's their fault, but it's important to remember that nobody has the right to hurt you because you have taken decisions or actions that they may not agree with.

Because HBV often happens in families and communities, it is really important to get support outside of the family to help keep you safe.

Why is this happening?

Your family or community may say you have brought 'shame' on them because:

- You are in a relationship with someone from a different religion/culture

- You do not want to marry someone your family wants you to, or you refuse a forced marriage (when someone is made to get married even though they don't want to)

- They do not agree with the clothes you wear and the way you dress

- You are gay, lesbian, bisexual or transgender.

However, all young people are individual, and just because you don't look or act like they want you to, doesn't mean they can force you to change.

What does HBV look like?

Crimes of 'honour' do not always include violence. Crimes committed in the name of 'honour' might include:

- Domestic violence – when someone hurts or bullies their boyfriend, girlfriend, partner, husband, wife, or family member

- Threats of violence

- Forced marriage

- Being held against your will or taken somewhere you don't want to go (this could include out of the country)

- Assault – when someone physically hurts you or threatens to physically hurt you

- Sexual abuse – making you do sexual things you don't want to including sex crimes such as sexual assault and rape

- Psychological abuse – such as being made to feel guilty, embarrassed or ashamed.

What can I do?

HBV can make you feel worried, sad or angry, and it may feel like you're trying to deal with this all on your own. However, lots of children and young people find that if they talk to someone it can help. Some things you can do:

- Tell an adult you trust – this could be a teacher, a family member, your youth worker, social worker or support worker. Think about talking to someone who is outside of the situation, who can advise you independently. It can be difficult to know how to have this conversation.

- Any form of violence and force is a crime, so think about reporting it to the police. If you're at immediate risk of getting hurt, call 999.

- With a safe adult, you could develop a safety plan that would help you choose how best to keep yourself safe.

- Talk to your friends. A good friend will listen to you and may help you speak to an adult.

If you are worried about a friend, the Victim Support website has some tips on how you can start the conversation and get them the right help.

Your questions answered about HBV

I'm a boy, can HBV affect me as well?

Although HBV is more commonly experienced by girls, it can happen to boys too. It often happens for the same reasons as girls. Boys may find it more difficult to talk about this, but it is just as serious and you should seek help.

If I report HBV, will it make it worse?

HBV isn't right and isn't legal. Victims are often too scared, shocked or worried about upsetting their family or community to speak out. For your own personal safety and that of the wider community, you should think seriously about reporting any incidents to the police, to prevent further crimes against you or others.

Have I brought shame on my family?

HBV is driven by a mistaken desire to protect the cultural or traditional beliefs of a family or community. No religion says that HBV is okay. It is never okay for somebody to upset, abuse, threaten or hurt you.

The above information is reprinted with kind permission from Victim Support.
© 2024 Victim Support

www.victimsupport.org.uk

So-called honour-based abuse

An extract.

So-called honour-based abuse can take a variety of forms, including female genital mutilation (FGM), forced marriage, honour killings, abandonment, breast flattening, and other forms of domestic abuse perpetrated in a perceived defence of 'honour.' It is the motivating factors behind the abuse that identifies it as honour-based, rather than the abuse itself, and that it is usually carried out with the collusion or approval from family and/or community members.

Whilst some forms of honour-based abuse are perceived and reported as occurring in certain communities, we heard it can occur within any community and is not a mainstream practice of any specific religion or culture. Perpetrators may be the victim's partner or former partner, parent or relative, a community member, or someone unknown to the victim – some perpetrators may be or have been victims themselves. It can also involve an international dimension. The majority of victims are female, though a significant minority of victims can be men, particularly in instances of forced marriage. Victims of honour-based abuse may face some or all of the following barriers to reporting their experiences:

- Fear that seeking support may lead to their family members being prosecuted;

- Fear that they may bring 'shame' or 'dishonour' upon their family if they seek help;

- Fear that seeking support may place them at greater risk;

- Fear that seeking support may require them to leave their family and community, leaving them isolated and depriving them of all roots and support networks;

- Finding it difficult in practice to access support, for example due to being controlled, or because they have been taken abroad;

- Not knowing that the act in question is wrong or illegal – the victim may regard it as normal community practice.

Prevalence

Unlike domestic abuse, there is no statutory definition of so-called honour-based abuse. However, the definition used by the Crown Prosecution Service (CPS) has been adopted by the National Police Chiefs' Council (NPCC) and the Government's Tackling Violence Against Women and Girls (VAWG) strategy published in July 2021. The CPS defines it as:

An incident or crime involving violence, threats of violence, intimidation, coercion or abuse (including psychological, physical, sexual, financial or emotional abuse) which has or may have been committed to protect or defend the honour of an individual, family and/or community for alleged or perceived breaches of the family and/or community's code of behaviour.

Data collection

In 2015, Her Majesty's Inspectorate of Constabulary (HMIC) investigated into the police response to honour-based violence, forced marriage, and FGM.

The inspectorate raised a number of concerns regarding data collection by the police. These included a lack of specific crime category for crimes of honour-based abuse, an inability of some forces to flag cases of honour- based abuse, and inaccurate recording of honour-based incidents or crimes. HMIC recommended:

The Home Office, in conjunction with the National Police Chiefs' Council, should develop an approach to the collection of data recorded by police forces in relation to HBV, [forced marriage] and FGM. Consideration should be given to this data being recorded as part of the Annual Data Return.

Since 2019–2020, the Home Office has collected and published data on honour-based abuse on a mandatory basis. Offences which are considered by the police to be motivated by so-called honour can be specifically flagged as such. The published data provides the overall number of honour-based abuse-related offences, including those which have not resulted in the recording of a notifiable crime. The data is broken down into offences of forced marriage, FGM, and 'other HBA-related tagged offences'.

In the year ending 31 March 2022, police in England and Wales recorded 2,887 offences related to honour-based abuse – a 6% increase on the previous year. In the period October 2022 to December 2022, the NHS had contact with 1,785 individual women and girls where FGM was identified.

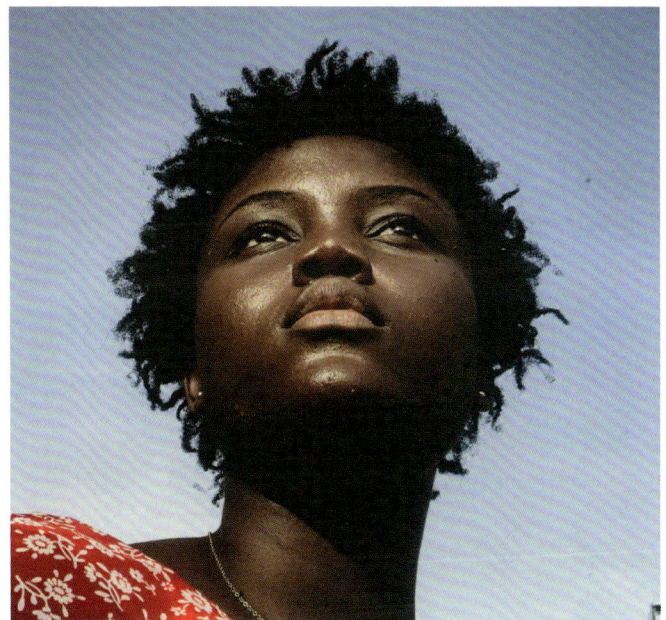

Types of so-called honour-based abuse

Submissions to the inquiry highlighted the wide range of forms that so-called honour-based abuse can take. Some of these forms are poorly understood, and not all are legally recognised. Below is a list of types of abuse which we received evidence about; this list is not intended to be comprehensive but rather to aid wider understanding and awareness.

Types of abuse include:

- Abandonment
- Abduction or kidnapping
- Abuse linked to faith or belief
- Acid attacks
- Blackmail
- Breast flattening or ironing
- Burning or scarring (whether for punishment or as part of a ritual)
- Child marriage/early marriage
- Coercive control including surveillance
- Death threats
- Domestic servitude and modern-day slavery
- Dowry abuse
- Emotional and psychological abuse
- Female genital mutilation (FGM)
- Financial/economic abuse
- Forced abortions, including for sex-selective purposes
- Forced feeding or other food-related abuse, including deprivation of food
- Forced marriage
- Forced suicide
- 'Honour' killings
- Imprisonment/deprivation of liberty
- Passport abuse
- Polygamy or temporary marriage
- Physical assault or abuse
- Rape including so-called 'revenge' rape or 'corrective' rape
- Shunning, disowning, and/or deliberately isolating the victim
- So-called conversion practices
- Trafficking
- Using the victim's children to carry out abuse
- Virginity testing and hymenoplasty
- Widow abuse.

Between April 2015 – when data collection on FGM was first mandated – and December 2022, NHS trusts and GP practices reported information about 32,740 individual women and girls who had experienced FGM.

In 2022, the Forced Marriage Unit, run jointly by the Home Office and the Foreign, Commonwealth and Development Office, dealt with a total of 302 cases (78% involved female victims and 22% involved male victims). The majority of victims (68%) were 25-years-old or younger, with 29% of victims aged 17 and under.

The data set out above only cover offences that were reported and recorded. Honour-based abuse is often a hidden crime and victims can be reluctant to bring the crimes to the attention of police or other authorities. As the Home Office recognises, 'the data, therefore, are likely to only represent a small proportion of the actual HBA offences committed'.

Education and RSHE

Schools can also play an important role in protecting children from honour-based abuse and educating them about harmful practices. From September 2020, all state schools have been required to consider statutory guidance on relationships, sex, and health education (RSHE). The statutory guidance outlines recommended topics to be taught as part of the RSHE curriculum in schools, including around honour-based abuse. However, schools have flexibility in how they choose to deliver RSHE and there is no standardised curriculum.

Both Yasmin Khan, Founder of the Halo Project, and Surwat Sohail, from domestic abuse charity Roshni, told us about their experiences working in schools. Ms Khan said she felt many schools send the message to young women at risk of honour-based abuse not to 'be silly' and to 'stand up to their parents'. Ms Sohail told us:

'I did sessions with 750 children, and 95% of them could not even identify what is a forced marriage, what is honour-based abuse, and why it is abuse. That is quite concerning.

Some of the participants in our "lived experience" session told us that although their abuse had started at school-age, their school had not recognised the abuse or taken action. Some felt this was a result of misplaced cultural sensitivities by the school; others felt the resources available to teachers were inadequate.'

19 July 2023

www.parliament.uk

What is honour-based abuse and how does it affect men?

In discussion with Karma Nirvana.

Founded by survivor Jasvinder Sanghera in 1993, Karma Nirvana is an award-winning national charity specialised in supporting victims of honour-based abuse and forced marriage. Operations Manager, Anup Manota, spoke to us about the complexities of honour-based abuse and the specific barriers male victims may face.

'People think it just affects a certain community or faith, and we're trying to eradicate that message,' Anup said. 'It could happen to anyone; it could be your neighbour, it could be your friend, it could be happening to your partner: it could be anyone.'

Honour-based abuse is not limited to any one community, but it is most common in communities with roots in South Asia, the Middle East, North Africa and East Africa. It is often reported from Muslim, Sikh, Hindu, Orthodox Jewish, and occasionally traveller communities.

In communities where honour-based abuse takes place, the family's views of 'honour' are considered extremely important and compromising that 'honour' can have severe consequences. The punishment for bringing dishonour to the family can range from physical and emotional abuse, to being disowned, and in some cases, even murder.

A survey from Safelives found that victims of honour-based abuse will experience abuse for at least five years before reporting. This is two years longer than domestic abuse victims. While studies show the majority of victims are women, men also experience honour-based abuse in a variety of complex ways.

The weight of social expectations

From a very young age, men in communities where honour-based abuse takes place are taught to be authoritative and macho. Male victims may struggle with accepting that they're being abused, because of these learned roles.

'There's a lot of manipulation going on, and I think for men, it's that they feel trapped,' Anup said. 'Because they're men, they shouldn't be feeling this way, according to what they've been taught.'

Anup explains that families often hold strong patriarchal values, which give men more freedom than women. For example, if a woman were to have a relationship with someone her parents disapproved of, she could be disowned or even killed.

In comparison, many male victims go to Karma Nirvana for help after 10–15 years, with two separate families – the one their parents forced on them and a secret one with a partner of their choosing. While they won't be killed for having two families, the prolonged stress and abuse affects their mental health over time.

'It can come out in different ways, such as complex post-traumatic stress disorder (PTSD), to the point where they're having mental breakdowns because it's become so overwhelming,' Anup explains.

In addition to marriage, Anup says parents have a 'checklist' they expect their sons to follow. They expect them to follow specific career paths, such as accountancy or engineering. Rejecting those expectations for less traditional paths could lead to abuse.

Sexuality, honour, and masculinity

'I think the biggest trigger with men is sexuality, where they're gay and their family have found out and now, they're forcing them into a marriage,' Anup said.

In cases of honour-based abuse, victims are seven times more likely to experience abuse from multiple perpetrators. Victims may experience abuse from parents, grandparents, siblings, extended family, and members of their community.

Because of that, many victims will ask not to be placed in areas where there may be members of their community, for their own safety. However, placing victims in areas away from their communities may present other risks.

One caller to Karma Nirvana escaped the abuse he had been suffering from his wife, since she found out about his sexuality. But after escaping, he and his children were placed in a city where they then suffered racist abuse.

'Not only was the man fleeing from honour-based abuse and homophobia, he was now also fleeing from racial abuse,' Anup said.

Another man went to Karma Nirvana in his mid-30s after five forced marriages. When he was 18-years-old, he told his parents he was gay. After that, they kept him from going to university and rushed to marry him off.

His marriages failed. So, the family tried again, and again. He faced constant physical and emotional abuse because of his family's views on honour and masculinity.

'In this man's case, he felt he wasted a lot of his years,' Anup said. 'Men need to know, that it's okay to be gay and be from, for example, a Muslim family. This shouldn't mean they are abused.'

The manipulation of faith

Manipulation of faith is common in honour-based abuse. Jasvinder questioned it as a child, but her mother would respond 'it's written,' in Punjabi. When she reached adulthood, she realised her mother had been lying.

That same manipulation is being used to justify honour-based abuse today. Anup says the less educated you are on your faith, the easier it is to believe what you're told.

'Faith in these communities has so much influence and dictation on how people live their lives,' Anup said. 'Using faith is a no-brainer for a lot of these perpetrators, because they know the victims will believe them.'

For victims of honour-based abuse, leaving is not an easy or clear-cut journey and many will return. Victims of honour-based abuse are often forced to choose between continuous abuse or losing their family.

'I think that's where we see a triggering time, where they'll just return home, because they can't cope with it,' Anup said. 'There is a loss of family and mourning for people that are alive.'

Reviewing gaps in support

According to data shared by Karma Nirvana, only three out of the 43 constabularies in England and Wales are prepared to respond to honour-based abuse.

The lack of response from the police isn't the only issue. Anup explains that a lack of understanding the differences between honour-based abuse and domestic abuse could also prevent support sector workers from giving survivors of honour-based abuse the support they need to continue living freely.

When victims of honour-based abuse make the decision to leave, counselling is essential, but some victims shared how counsellors have asked problematic questions such as, 'why didn't you just ring your mum up and tell her how you feel?'

In order to support victims of honour-based abuse, we need to spread awareness and engage with communities. Anup highlights a need for collaboration between charities. Often, cases are referred to Karma Nirvana just because of the ethnicity of the victim, not because they are experiencing honour-based abuse.

By having stronger communications and increased awareness of specialist services, more victims of domestic and honour-based abuse could be helped. Let's talk about honour-based abuse.

9 September 2020

Consider...
Why do you think that men take longer to seek help for 'honour-based' abuse?

Design
Design a poster or leaflet for male victims of 'honour-based' abuse. Remember to include details of charities or organisations that they can go to for help and advice.

Write
Write a definition of the words honour and dishonour.

www.respect.org.uk
www.karmanirvana.org.uk

Reports of 'honour-based' abuse increased following lockdowns and change to police recording rules

An article by The Conversation.

By Sadiq Bhanbhro, Senior Research Fellow on Public Health and Gender-Based Violence, Sheffield Hallam University

Cases of so-called honour-based abuse (HBA) are on the rise in England and Wales.

Home Office figures show 2,905 HBA offences in 2022-23 – an increase of 1% in the year ending March 2023 from the year before. This is a rise of 10% since 2020-21.

It has been mandatory for police in England and Wales to record crimes often referred to as 'honour-based' since 2019. Between 2016 and 2020, the number recorded rose by 81%.

This mandatory reporting may be behind some of the increase in offences. But the pandemic lockdowns also provided abusers with greater opportunity to offend. What's more, there may be many cases of HBA that go unreported.

There are a variety of harmful practices categorised as HBA. These include forced marriages, sexual, psychological and economic abuse, female genital mutilation, and honour killings. These crimes are committed by people seeking to defend or restore the honour of a person or social group, such as a family, clan, caste, kin group or community.

A global issue

It is a global issue happening across different cultures and communities, although some areas are considered more affected, such as the Middle East and south Asia.

While such crimes can affect anyone, women and girls are more likely to be targeted. In the UK, it is particularly prevalent among young girls. In 2022, the Forced Marriage Unit handled 302 cases: 78% of the victims were female, while 22% were male. Over half of the victims were 21 or younger.

My research with communities in the UK and abroad indicates that the ideology that triggers this harmful behaviour towards family members is that women and girls are considered carriers of family honour, and a precious social resource.

Given the social, cultural and economic value of family honour that lies with women and girls, social groups have rules and practices to protect the value they have placed in honour.

For example, if a young woman marries without her family or parents' consent, this act would be considered dishonourable for the family. This young woman's behaviour can trigger gossip about her family's reputation, showing that the family is exposed to dishonour and shame in its concerned social group. As a result, the family, particularly the male members, will attempt to restore the family honour.

The actions and behaviour taken to protect or restore family honour in this way are context-specific. The action could range from a harsh warning to murder, and any harmful behaviour in between, such as threatening, stalking, harassing or forcing her to leave her husband.

Impact of lockdown

However, this type of crime is often not reported to authorities because victims hesitate to come forward. HBA thrives in secrecy and fear. The COVID-19 lockdowns and associated restrictions created an environment which made it easier for perpetrators to commit offences and more difficult for survivors to seek help.

The national helpline for HBA saw a significant decline in calls about forced marriage following the government's order to stay home on March 23 2020. The helpline saw a peak in contacts in May 2020, following the easing of some restrictions – and another rise when schools reopened in September 2020.

The number of reported cases has also increased because of the implementation of official recording methods, which has slightly improved its visibility. The murder of Banaz Mahmod in 2006 drew attention to honour crimes in the UK, and there has been a gradual increase in the awareness of these offences.

But political cultural sensitivities may be getting in the way of tackling HBA. For example, it has been alleged that the Crown Prosecution Service may have avoided tackling such crimes for fear of creating 'unrest' in communities.

Similarly, police may have been nervous about investigating sexual abuse in ethnic minority communities for fear of being labelled racist.

Key Facts

- In the year 2022-23 there were 2,905 reported cases of so-called honour-abuse.

- Many cases of HBA go unreported.

- In 2022, the Forced Marriage Unit handled 302 cases: 78% of the victims were female, while 22% were male.

- Half of the victims of forced marriage are under 21.

The UK parliament's Women and Equalities Committee recently carried out an inquiry into so-called honour-based abuse, reviewing evidence submitted by several witnesses and experts, including myself. The committee called for the creation of a legal definition of HBA.

A shared, statutory definition would increase awareness and also reduce the hypersensitivity attached to HBA that frames it as a cultural problem of certain communities, which often prevents state agencies from acting and prosecuting such violent crimes.

Additionally, a legal definition for HBA would contribute to social and professional understanding, help to improve data collection and ultimately assist in bringing more perpetrators to justice.

The government has rejected the committee's recommendation for a statutory definition of HBA, however. This is a missed opportunity to take a decisive step forward in the fight against this kind of crime.

29 November 2023

Write

Why do you think that the COVID-19 lockdown had an impact on the number of reported cases?

Write

Currently, there is no statutory definition of HBA. In pairs, write what you think the definition should be.

THE CONVERSATION

'Honour-based' abuse in England increases 60% in two years

Global political influence may make assault and forced marriage more frequent and severe, say experts.

By Haroon Siddique, Legal Affairs Correspondent

The number of 'honour-based' abuse offences recorded by English police forces has increased by more than 60% in two years, figures suggest, with concerns voiced that increased polarisation is partly to blame.

Data from 26 out of 39 constabularies approached showed that there were 2,594 cases of 'honour-based' abuse – which includes forced marriage, rape, death threats, and assault – in 2022, compared with 1,599 in 2020.

The increase, which was even more pronounced since 2016 (up 193%), may be partly explained by more victims coming forward and improved identification of offences by police – but other factors are also believed to be at work.

Imran Khodabocus, a director at the Family Law Company, based in south-west England, which sourced the figures, said: 'In cases like this, you can't minimise the impact of global political and social issues. In my experience, some people are becoming more rigid in their thinking and this is creating more instances where they feel they must defend their, or their families', honour.'

He said the figures reflected his experience that honour-based offences 'are not just rising, but getting more severe.' The Metropolitan Police, West Midlands and Greater Manchester forces recorded the highest rates of honour-based abuse in 2021 and 2022.

Across the two years, the Metropolitan Police recorded 1,213 cases, including 514 cases of violence. There were two attempted murders, 32 rapes, 310 cases of forced marriage, and 49 cases of female genital mutilation.

Greater Manchester police's tally of 729 cases included 42 of rape, 65 assaults causing actual bodily harm, 56 forced marriage offences, 104 of assault and battery and 153 instances of controlling or coercive behaviour in an intimate or family relationship.

West Midlands recorded 729 cases including 115 of coercive behaviour in an intimate relationship, 27 of rape, 19 forced marriages, and 90 threats to kill.

Khodabocus said that delays in the family courts were exacerbating the problem.

'There is not the same drive to clear chronic backlogs in these courts as we have seen recently in the criminal courts,' he said. 'This means many cases I act in are taking at least nine to 12 months to be resolved, leaving families and particularly children in a vulnerable position. For many of the cases I act in, a lack of court interpreters is also creating significant delays to cases.'

He expressed surprise that he was seeing more forced marriage cases, given that just over a year ago the legal age of marriage increased in the UK from 16 to 18 in an attempt to address the problem.

A spokesperson from women's rights organisation Iranian & Kurdish Women's Rights (IKWRO) said it was deeply troubled by the increase. They added: 'The observation that global political and social factors contribute to the polarisation of views and exacerbate "honour-based" abuse is particularly noteworthy. It highlights the intersectionality of this issue with broader societal dynamics and underscores the need for nuanced approaches in addressing it.

'IKWRO echoes Imran's call for more education and training for authorities to recognise the signs of "honour-based" abuse and respond effectively working collaboratively with specialist organisations.'

They agreed that family court delays were 'leaving victims, particularly children, in vulnerable situations for extended periods'.

A government spokesperson highlighted the increase in the legal age of marriage and the creation of a dedicated forced marriage unit to support victims, adding: 'Meanwhile our courts are running at full throttle delivering justice for victims and holding offenders to account.'

7 April 2024

Key Facts

- The number of 'honour-based' abuse offences has increased by more than 60% in two years

- The police forces with the highest rates of HBA were: The Metropolitan police, West Midlands police and Greater Manchester police.

Harmful Practices

Chapter 2

What is FGM?

What exactly is female genital mutilation?

Female genital mutilation (FGM) is a practice in which the female genital organs are intentionally altered or injured for non-medical reasons. Predominantly carried out on young girls, the practice has cultural, religious, and social implications, and has a lifelong impact on the health and wellbeing of millions of women and girls worldwide.

UNICEF estimates that around 230 million women and girls have undergone female genital mutilation.

It's deeply embedded within various cultures and societies across the world, but is most common in Africa.

FGM is also referred to as female circumcision or cutting, and by other terms, such as Sunna, gudniin, halalays, tahur, megrez and khitan, among others.

The procedure is often carried out by people with no medical experience, known as the 'cutter', using unsafe equipment, such as knives, razors, glass and sharpened stones. The equipment is often used on multiple people, and is not clean or sterile.

The victims are often forcibly restrained, and receive no anaesthetic or antiseptic treatment.

FGM is a form of child abuse and is a criminal offence in the UK.

The different types of FGM

FGM is not a single procedure, but rather a range of practices that vary widely from one culture to another. It has various forms, primarily categorized into four major types:

- Type I (Clitoridectomy): This involves the partial or total removal of the clitoris and sometimes the prepuce (the fold of skin surrounding the clitoris).

- Type II (Excision): Here, the clitoris and the labia minora are partially or totally removed, sometimes including the labia majora.

- Type III (Infibulation): This is the narrowing of the vaginal opening by creating a covering seal, which is formed by cutting and repositioning the labia.

- Type IV: This encompasses all other harmful procedures to the female genitalia for non-medical purposes, like pricking, piercing, incising, scraping, or cauterising.

It's essential to understand that all these practices present serious health risks and are recognised internationally as a violation of human rights.

Types of FGM

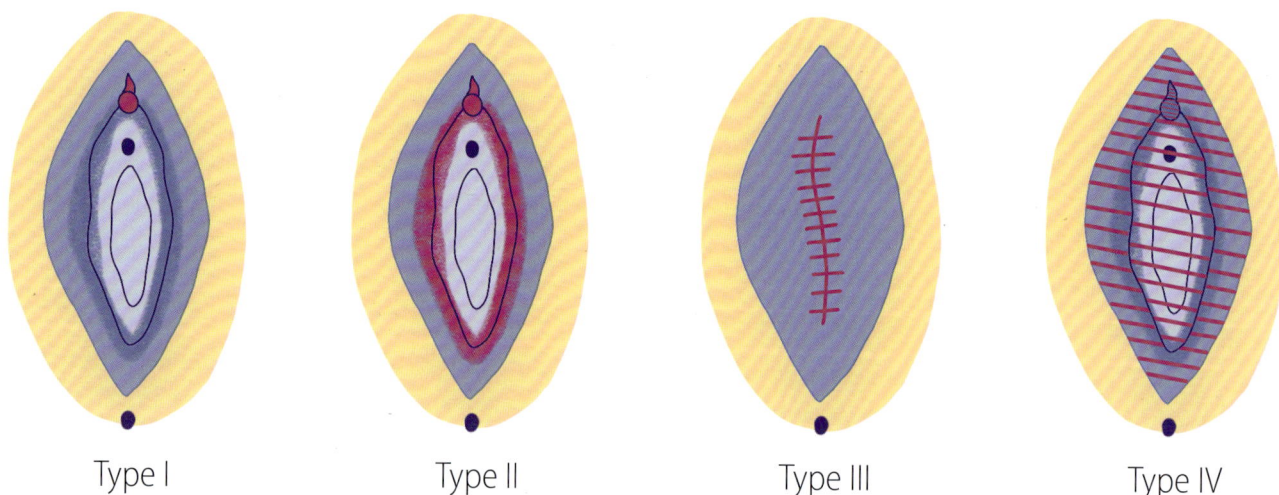

Type I   Type II   Type III   Type IV

■ Removal   ≢ Stitches   Any other injury including pricking, burning, piercing, and scraping

Why does FGM take place?

FGM is often motivated by a complex mix of cultural, social, and sometimes misguided religious beliefs. Here are some reasons:

- Tradition: In some communities, FGM is perceived as a rite of passage for girls into womanhood.

- Religious beliefs: FGM is often incorrectly linked to certain religious practices.

- Preservation of virginity: It's falsely believed that FGM helps maintain a girl's 'purity' before marriage.

- Male sexual pleasure: A prevalent misconception is that FGM enhances male sexual pleasure.

None of these reasons excuse the practice – understanding them is merely the first step in dismantling the structures that support FGM.

When does FGM take place?

FGM can happen at different times in a girl or woman's life. It's most commonly done before puberty; however, it can also be done just before marriage, during pregnancy, after giving birth, or even when a woman is widowed.

Where is FGM common?

FGM is a global issue, with particular prevalence in parts of Africa, the Middle East, and Asia. It may also be encountered among certain immigrant communities in Europe, North America, and Australia – reflecting cultural practices from their countries of origin that have continued despite migration.

Health consequences

Remember, FGM is a harmful procedure with no health benefits. Short-term health risks can include severe pain, infection, and even death. Long-term consequences incorporate chronic pain, sexual health problems, and psychological trauma. FGM violates a woman's right to health, physical integrity, and, in extreme cases, to life itself.

The repercussions of FGM on health are grave:

- Immediate risks: Severe pain, shock, haemorrhage (bleeding), tetanus (a bacterial infection that causes muscle stiffness and spasms), sepsis (a life-threatening condition caused by infection), urine retention (inability to urinate), and even death.

- Long-term outcomes: Chronic pain, infections, cysts and infertility are all too common among women who have undergone FGM. Also, women can experience difficulty passing urine, painful and prolonged periods due to the vaginal closure. Complications during childbirth and increased risk of newborn deaths also occur more frequently in these cases.

- Mental health: FGM often leads to long-term psychological trauma, including depression, anxiety, and post-traumatic stress disorder.

FGM and the law

In the UK, FGM is illegal. Plain and simple.

The UK implemented laws that make FGM illegal in 1985 with the Prohibition of Female Circumcision Act 1985. However, this was updated in 2003. It's a crime to conduct FGM in the UK or to take a UK resident abroad for FGM. Moreover, any

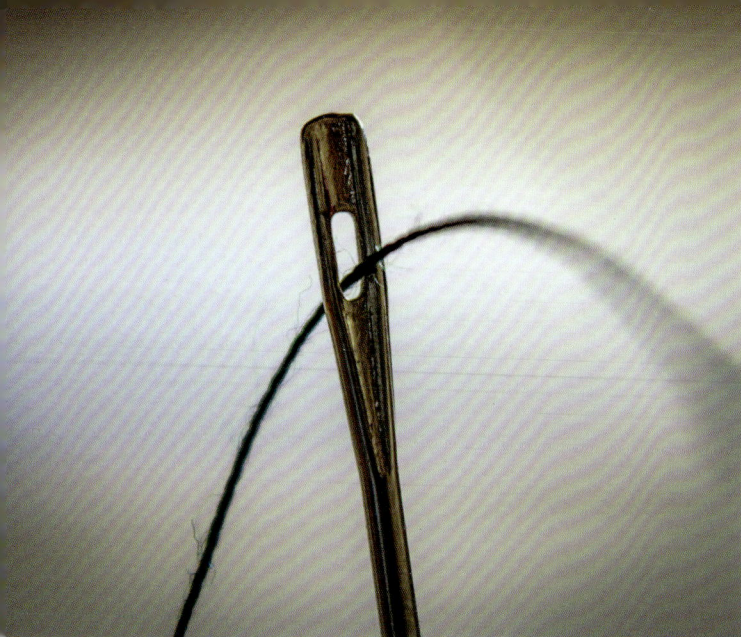

knowledge of FGM practices where an at-risk girl under 18 is involved must be reported to the police. Individuals who fail to report this knowledge can also be held accountable.

The Female Genital Mutilation Act 2003, updated by the Serious Crime Act 2015, provides the framework:

- It's criminal to perform FGM in the UK or assist a girl to mutilate her own genitalia.

- Taking a girl abroad to have FGM performed is also criminal – this is known as 'FGM tourism'.

- Professionals, like teachers and health workers, must report known cases of FGM in under-18s to the police.

Protective measures are in place for a reason – to keep girls safe.

Tackling FGM

So, what can we do to halt FGM? Educate, empower, and engage.

1. Knowledge is power: Understanding the dangers of FGM is fundamental.

2. Community involvement: Change starts at home – having open conversations within communities can challenge the traditions that support FGM.

3. Legislation: Strong laws are the backbone of protecting girls and women from FGM.

4. Support services: Counselling, medical help, and support groups play a critical role in healing for survivors of FGM.

Education is not just about absorbing information; it's about transforming perspectives and practices.

Scared? Victimised?

If you or someone you know is in danger of FGM or has been a victim, help is available. In the UK, you can reach out to the NSPCC FGM Helpline at 0800 028 3550 or help@nspcc.org. uk, or even dial 999 if it's an emergency.

Remember, you're not alone, and you have the right to receive help.

In conclusion

Female genital mutilation is a complex and deeply entrenched practice. As we delve deeply into this widely misunderstood topic, let us face it head-on, in our classrooms, in our homes, and within our communities.

It's with knowledge, curiosity, and a deep dedication to human rights that we can begin to build a world free of FGM. Always remember, censoring or shying away from these topics might save a moment of awkwardness, but initiating open conversations can save lives.

While the intricacies of FGM might seem overwhelming, each conversation we have about it opens a door towards ending this practice. By fostering environments where tough topics can be approached with sensitivity and respect – and by empowering ourselves and others to speak up against injustice – we can make a difference.

So let's challenge ourselves to be part of the change, using our voices and platforms to spread knowledge and advocate for those who may still be silenced.

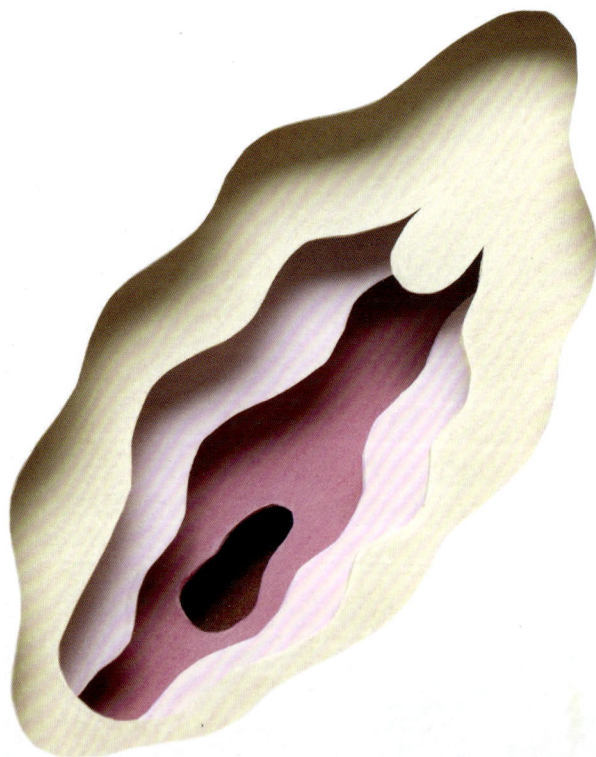

FGM is leading cause of death in some nations, study finds

'Change in patriarchal attitudes often lags behind other societal change – an important first step would be for FGM to be made illegal in the countries where it is within the law,' report author says.

By Maya Oppenheim, Women's Correspondent

Female genital mutilation is a leading cause of death in the nations where it is carried out, according to a damning new study.

Researchers found a 50% surge in the number of girls undergoing FGM causes over an estimated 44,000 excess deaths of women and young girls each year in countries where the practice occurs.

FGM, internationally recognised as a human rights violation, refers to any procedure that intentionally alters female genital organs for non-medical reasons. The procedure, which can cause a lifetime of severe health problems and pain, is often carried out without anaesthesia.

Some 'girls die from blood loss or infection as a direct result of the procedure', the NHS states.

The new study, carried out at by the University of Birmingham and Exeter, discovered FGM amounts for more deaths in some nations than any cause apart from respiratory infections, or malaria and enteric infections – which generally stem from consuming contaminated food or water.

Researchers, who looked at the numbers of girls subjected to FGM in Benin, Mali, Burkina Faso, Chad, Guinea, Ethiopia, Cameroon, Côte d'Ivoire, Egypt, Kenya, Niger, Sierra Leone, Nigeria, Senegal, and Tanzania, noted FGM is legal in five of the 28 countries where it is most performed.

Professor James Rockey, the report's co-author, said: 'Our findings show that FGM is a leading cause of death amongst girls and young women in countries where it is practised, but lasting change requires changing attitudes towards FGM in these communities.

'There is cause for optimism, as work on non-communicable diseases shows effective interventions are possible, but change in patriarchal attitudes often lags behind other societal change – an important first step would be for FGM to be made illegal in the countries where it is within the law, given that legal change can lead to cultural change.'

Researchers, whose findings were published in *Nature Scientific Reports*, argued FGM should be outlawed in Mali, Chad, Malawi, Sierra Leone, and Liberia, as well as warning measures must be bolstered to tackle FGM in nations where it takes place.

Around the world, over 200 million women and girls are estimated to have endured FGM – with the World Health Organisation (WHO) estimating the total cost of medical treatment which women and girls access after being subjected to FGM as $1.4 billion in 2018.

The NHS notes FGM can cause perpetual pain, recurrent infections, which can trigger infertility, bleeding, cysts, abscesses, incontinence, and pain during sex.

The practice can also cause 'depression, flashbacks, and self-harm, and problems during labour and childbirth, which can be life-threatening for mother and baby,' the NHS adds, as well as stating FGM can also cause 'reduced sexual desire and a lack of pleasurable sensation'.

18 August 2023

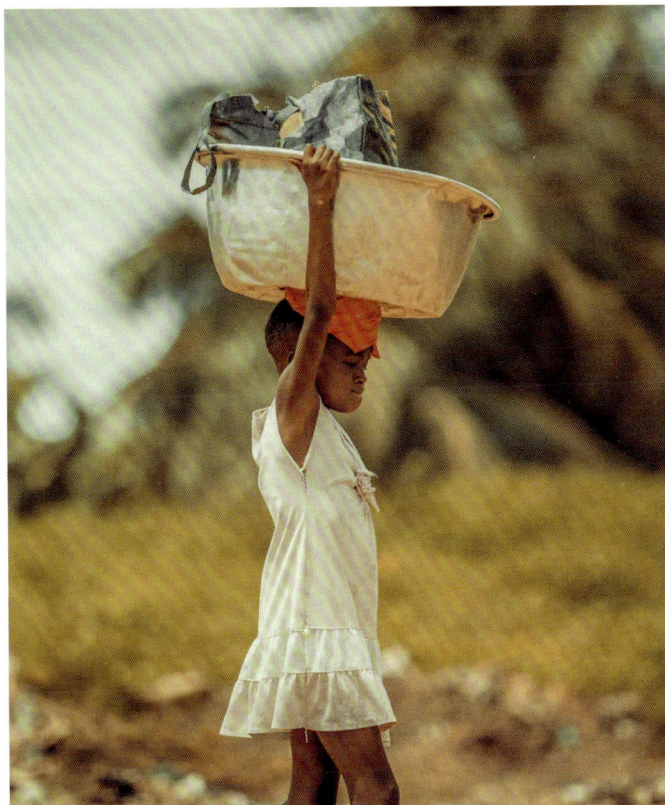

British Somalis and FGM: 'everybody is a suspect – you are guilty until proven innocent'

An article from The Conversation.

By Saffron Karlsen, Senior lecturer in Social Research, University of Bristol, Christina Pantazis, Professor of Zemiology, University of Bristol, Magda Mogilnicka, Research Associate in the School of Sociology, Politics and International Studies, University of Bristol & Natasha Carver, Lecturer in International Criminology, University of Bristol

Female genital mutilation (FGM), whereby the female genitals are deliberately injured or changed for non-medical reasons, is considered by the UN to be a 'global concern'.

International organisations often report statistical evidence that 98% of women and girls in Somalia/Somaliland have undergone FGM.

Because of this international evidence, girls born to Somali parents living in the UK are considered to be at high risk of experiencing FGM. Yet research shows that attitudes towards FGM change dramatically following migration and therefore girls in the UK are unlikely to be put through this procedure.

Concern over the practice of FGM has led the UK government to create policies intended to protect girls at risk. Known as FGM safeguarding, these policies require professionals – such as teachers, healthcare or youth workers – to report to the police any concerns that a child has had, or could be at risk of, FGM.

Our research presents the views of Somali families living in Bristol with experience of FGM safeguarding. Our findings were collected during six focus groups with 30 Somali men, women and young adults during the summer of 2018.

Somalis in our study were committed to ending FGM, but felt detrimentally affected by existing approaches to FGM safeguarding. A sense of the exploitation of a disempowered community pervaded our discussions.

Constant safeguarding

Many of the people we spoke with felt that FGM safeguarding led those in positions of authority and trust to put pressure on families to comply with demands that are stigmatising, unjustified and contrary to their rights as British citizens.

Women experienced FGM safeguarding repeatedly in routine health visits – with midwives, GPs and health visitors. They felt that medical staff prioritised getting information for government FGM statistics over their health needs – without considering the trauma this could cause.

The women spoke about how health professionals repeatedly 'put salt on the wound' caused by their own experiences of FGM through relentless and insensitive questioning. In response, participants reported avoiding or being scared to access medical care. One of the women we spoke to told us:

Before they cared about your health and how the child was feeling. Now it's just FGM.

FGM safeguarding in schools usually occurred when parents asked to take their children on holiday during term time. Instead of appropriate guidelines being applied, participants believed that Somalis in Bristol were referred to social services by schools as a matter of course – regardless of any identified level of risk to their children.

These experiences stigmatised, traumatised and alienated Somali families, damaging their trust in schools. As one of the people we spoke with explained:

I thought that safeguarding was when a child is in danger. But for us it was just because we were Somali.

Referrals to social services frequently led to unannounced home visits by social workers and (sometimes uniformed) police. These visits scared and traumatised children and received particular condemnation from the people in our study.

Safeguarding officers were described as failing to respect people's rights to privacy and autonomy. The people described how officers would separate and interrogate family members – including children – and physically search property without justification.

Everyone a suspect

Participants repeatedly said that FGM safeguarding treated Somalis like criminals. They felt distrusted and that their needs were ignored. There was a sense that the whole Somali community was targeted unfairly.

They also described the safeguarding policy as inherently racist and felt that wider political and media debates on FGM directly contributed to their personal experiences of racist violence. As one of the participants said:

Everybody is a suspect. You are guilty until you are proven innocent.

The people in our study said that their experience of FGM safeguarding had undermined their strong sense of being British and made them feel like they were living

in a hostile environment. They also described the ways in which the important work being done by Somali activists to reduce FGM was being ignored and this fed into negative stereotypes about Somali culture.

People in our study felt that these heavy-handed approaches were encouraged by incorrect beliefs that FGM was still popular among the British Somali population. Our participants explained that people living in the UK were much less supportive of FGM than was assumed. This view is supported by other research in this area. This questions the value of using FGM statistics from Somalia/Somaliland as the basis for understanding FGM risk to Somali people living the UK. One of the people we spoke to said:

We are trying to find our identity as British Somalis and we don't want FGM to be part of that.

This is why a government review of the statistical evidence underpinning FGM safeguarding policies is urgently needed to find better ways to establish FGM risk.

Healthcare workers must also address evidence which highlights that FGM safeguarding in medical settings can lead to poorer care and traumatise FGM victims.

Similarly, schools must ensure that all approaches to FGM safeguarding are in accordance with existing guidance. Home visits must also only be carried out once reasonable risk has been identified – and conducted in a way that doesn't feel distressing, criminalising or coercive in nature.

Our research shows that FGM safeguarding services in Britain could be doing great harm, even to the people they intend to protect. Only by working together can services be developed that work for everyone.

18 March 2020

THE CONVERSATION

Woman guilty of handing over British child, 3, for female genital mutilation in Kenya

A court heard the girl cried for the 'whole night' after the procedure.

By Amy-Clare Martin, Crime Correspondent

A British woman has been found guilty of handing over a three-year-old who was subjected to female genital mutilation in a legal first.

Jurors were told Amina Noor, 39, took the toddler, who cannot be named for legal reasons, to Kenya in 2006 where the procedure was carried out.

A court heard the girl, who was not told what would happen to her, cried for the 'whole night' after the procedure.

On Thursday, Noor was found guilty of assisting a person to mutilate a girl's genitalia while outside the UK, contrary to the FGM Act of 2003, following a week-long trial at the Old Bailey. She was granted conditional bail and is due to be sentenced on 20 December.

Prosecutors have said the conviction, which is the first of its kind, sends a 'clear message' over the practice of FGM, which is 'shrouded in secrecy'. Noor is also only the second person to be found guilty of any offence under FGM laws, which brings a maximum sentence of up to 14 years in prison.

During the trial, prosecutor Deanna Heer KC said Ms Noor travelled by tuk-tuk to a clinic at a private house in the east African country, where the girl was taken into a room on her own by a woman whose medical qualifications were not known.

The girl, who was born in Britain, was not told what would happen to her or was 'too young to understand'.

'Whilst they were there, she took [the girl] to the house of Kenyan woman, where [the girl] was subjected to female genital mutilation (FGM),' she told the court.

Afterwards, the toddler was 'quiet' but later cried the whole night, complaining of pain when she went to the toilet.

The incident was not reported until 2018, when the girl – then aged 16 – confided in an English teacher who contacted the authorities.

During a medical examination at a London hospital in 2019, doctors confirmed the girl's clitoris had been fully removed.

Jurors heard the defendant was born in Somalia and moved to Kenya at the age of eight during the civil war in her home country. She was 16 when she came to the United Kingdom and was later granted British citizenship.

The court was told that 94% of women of Somali origin living in Kenya undergo FGM, according to United Nations' figures.

In a police interview in 2019, Noor, who denied the charge, said she had expected the child to undergo 'Sunnah', which she said was the insertion of a needle in the genitalia to draw blood, but insisted she did not know her clitoris would be removed.

'She said that it was a quick procedure and that although [the child] had cried when it was carried out, she was happy and able to run around and play afterwards,' Deer told the court.

However, she said did not check the child's wound, 'nor did she want to', the court heard.

Giving evidence, Noor, from Harrow, northwest London, told jurors she feared she would have been 'disowned and cursed' if she did not hand over the child.

She said: 'I didn't know whether this was going to be something that is harming (the girl) but I did not want to allow it whatever it might be. I was told I would be cursed if I refuse.'

Senior crown prosecutor Patricia Strobino, who works in the CPS London Complex Casework Unit, hailed Noor's conviction as sending a 'clear message' on FGM, and urged other survivors to come forward. She said: 'This kind of case will hopefully encourage potential victims and survivors of FGM to come forward, safe in the knowledge that they are supported, believed and also are able to speak their truth about what's actually happened to them.

'It will also send a clear message to those prospective defendants or people that want to maintain this practice that it doesn't matter whether they assist or practise or maintain this practice within the UK, or overseas, they are likely to be prosecuted.'

She added: 'Part of the challenge of this type of offence is the fact that these types of offences occur in secrecy.

'Within specific communities within the UK, although these offences and practices are prevalent, it's often very difficult to get individuals to come forward to explain the circumstances of what's happened to them because there was a fear that they may be excluded or pushed away or shunned, isolated from their community.'

In a statement outside court, Detective Superintendent Andy Furphy, of the Metropolitan Police, said: 'I hope this conviction demonstrates the lengths we will go to, to enforce the law on female genital mutilation.

'If you reside in the UK and take, arrange or facilitate a child to be taken out of the country for this barbaric crime, no matter where it takes place in the world, we can convict you.'

Responding to landmark case, an FGM campaigner called for urgent updates to outdated statistics for women and girls affected in England and Wales. Figures dating from 2014 estimate there are 137,000 impacted by FGM.

Nimco Ali, FGM survivor and cofounder of Five Foundation, a global partnership to end FGM, said: 'I underwent FGM at age 7, so I know this girl's pain. When I told my teacher in Manchester, very little could be done to help me or others like me, who were affected by FGM.

'Thankfully, things have changed so much in the last decades, following the work we have done to improve laws and policies, and get this issue out of the shadows and onto the front pages of national media.

'It is incredible that the mandatory reporting by teachers and health care professionals – that we have fought hard for – is starting to pay off. A girl was obviously failed. She was let down by the system, but she got some form of justice today, thanks to the policies that we now have in place.'

She added: 'We have to address FGM in the UK and everywhere by working together to address the root causes of the issue. The next step is getting a clearer sense of the number of women and girls who are affected here.'

26 October 2023

Key Facts

- An estimated 137,000 women and girls have been impacted by FGM in England and Wales.

- 94% of women of Somali origin living in Kenya undergo FGM, according to United Nations' figures.

- There is no up-to-date figure of how many women and girls in the UK have been affected by FGM.

www.independent.co.uk

Breast flattening

Breast flattening is an age-old tradition, practised in certain parts of Africa. It is the pounding and massaging of a girl's breasts to delay breast development. In the UK it is child abuse. Read this guide to find out more.

What is breast flattening and breast ironing?

Breast flattening (often called breast ironing) is the pounding and massaging of a young girl's breasts, to prevent and stunt breast growth. It is usually carried out by pressing, massaging, or pounding the breasts using hard or heated objects.

Why does it happen?

Breast flattening is traditional practice in parts of West Africa. It is typically arranged or performed by the girl's mother, to make the girl less attractive to males by delaying the signs that the girl is maturing into a young woman. Reasons for this include, protecting the girl from sexual harassment and rape. It is also carried out to discourage pre-marital sex, unwanted pregnancy, and prevent early marriage. Often one of the drivers is that the mother will want her daughter to avoid pregnancy so that they receive an education.

Where does it occur?

Breast flattening is widespread in Cameroon and also takes place throughout other parts of Africa. Countries include: Benin, Chad, Côte d'Ivoire, Guinea-Bissau, Guinea, Kenya, Nigeria, Togo. There have also been reports that the practice can be found further south – in Zimbabwe and South Africa.

How prevalent is it?

Because breast flattening is a hidden practice, it is difficult to establish how prevalent it really is. The UN estimate that nearly 4 million girls are affected, whilst other research identifies that in Cameroon alone, 1 in 4 girls has undergone the process. This would significantly increase the UN estimate.

Who's at risk?

The practice usually starts when a girl begins to develop breasts, generally affecting pubescent girls aged between 8 and 12 years of age.

How is it carried out?

There are several methods to iron or flatten the breast, often determined by the area or region where it takes place. A pestle or grinding stone are the most commonly used tools. Typically, the preferred tool will be heated in a fire or boiling water until very hot, then applied to the breast. The object will then be pressed, pounded, and massaged into the breast for several minutes. Once the object cools, it is placed back into the fire and reapplied when hot enough. Once the massaging has finished, the breasts are often tightly bandaged or bound by a belt (or other restrictive material). The pounding or pressing can continue daily, sometimes twice a day, for several months until the breasts have dropped or not developed.

Other tools include:

* Bananas
* Towels or cloth
* Leaves thought to have medicinal and healing qualities
* Coconut shell
* Spatulas, spoons, or other similar wooded objects
* Foodstuff – fufu, seeds, fruits, nuts.

Whilst normally performed by the child's mother, other female family members can perform or assist in the practice. In some cases, male members of the family, healers, elders, and other members of the community may become involved. Given that the act is excruciatingly painful, it is likely that the child will need to be restrained.

What are the health implications?

Apart from the severe pain, the practice causes:

- Burning and scarring

- Long term malformation or disappearance of the breasts

- Abscesses

- Life threatening infections

- Tissue damage

- Interference with breastfeeding

- Mastitis

- Psychological problems – anxiety, fear, depression, PTSD.

Whilst there is limited information available about the long-term effects of breast ironing, experts warn that it could lead to the development of cysts, and skin and breast cancer.

Key Facts

- The UN estimate that nearly 4 million girls have undergone breast flattening.

- 1 in 4 girls in Cameroon have undergone the process.

- Breast flattening is usually carried out between 8 and 12 years old.

Does it happen in the UK?

Despite occasional stories in the British press with headlines like 'hundreds of UK girls subject to breast ironing,' no one knows how widespread it is in the UK. It is a hidden crime, taking place in private and where the victim is unlikely to report their mother or family member. Whilst there are no official police or government figures, it is widely accepted that it has been brought to the UK and is practised amongst those communities that have now settled here.

There has been concern from the Home Office that safeguarding professionals might be reluctant to engage and challenge families and communities, because of cultural sensitivities. This may have happened in some cases, but rather than throw around unhelpful comments, it would be more beneficial for the government to launch an awareness campaign aimed at safeguarding professionals. They could also look at whether specific legislation is required, for whilst there is no specific law on breast ironing, it is child abuse. If practised in the UK, the perpetrators are subject to other UK laws – assault (likely to be grievous bodily harm) and child cruelty. A campaign and some investment by the government, would go a long way to empowering professionals to be confident around identification, the law and the safeguarding measures they need to take.

15 July 2023

Consider...

Breast flattening/ironing is often carried out by mothers to 'protect' their daughters. What other non-harmful things could they do to help protect their daughters from early marriage and unwanted pregnancy?

www.safeguardinghub.co.uk

Breast ironing: a harmful practice that spans generations

The cocks crowed, signifying morning was nigh.

Hope shuddered as she thought of what awaited her.

Her developing breasts throbbed with excruciating pain, worsened hours ago when her mama had pounded them with hot stones.

She'd cried and pled as mama pounded and auntie held her, but it was useless.

They said they were doing it for her, they didn't want the men to desire her, but Hope felt none of their love.

All she felt was the pain.

And she saw the scars she knew would never leave.

She heard mama's footsteps. It was time.

This was her daily routine, one that began when she'd clocked nine and the breasts started to show.

She sobbed, wishing herself away from this hidden ritual.

No one could hear her, no one could save her.

Hope may not be real but what she suffered – breast ironing – is. This is the reality for many girls.

Breast ironing is an action carried out to stop the development of breasts. It is carried out by using hot objects like stones, paddles, spatulas, and brooms to massage, pound, and press the breasts flat. Sometimes, belts or bandages are used to bind the breasts. This act is usually carried out by mothers, female relatives, shamans, and, rarely, the victim.

I first came to know of this practice when I stumbled across a report by Aljazeera, detailing this cruel act that is ongoing within refugee communities in Ogoja, Nigeria – my country. The report explained that this act is carried out by refugee Cameroonian mothers because of the high levels of sexual harassment and assault to which female refugees are exposed. It is done in the hope that their daughters will become less desirable to men.

According to the United Nations, 3.8 million girls in the world today are affected by breast ironing

Breast ironing culture, also known as breast flattening, is widespread in African countries like Cameroon, Guinea-Bissau, Chad, Benin, and Togo. It is most prevalent in Cameroon, with the number of girls who have been subjected to it estimated at around 1.3 million! However, it is not only prevalent in African countries. Came Women and Girls Development Organisation estimate that every year, 1000 girls aged 9–15 across the UK are victims of breast ironing!

The reasons behind the practice are meant to 'protect' girls

Mothers perform this act because they believe that no breasts will make their daughters less attractive to the opposite sex, thereby warding off sexual advances. These mothers ignore their daughters' pain as they have the intention of 'protecting' them from rape, sexual harassment, early marriage.

Nonetheless, it remains a misguided intention because breast ironing only exposes girls to extreme pain, psychological damage, infections, cancer, and inverted nipples.

What's being done against breast ironing?

Breast ironing does not receive as much attention as it should. In Cameroon, where it is rampant, anti-breast-ironing laws are non-existent. In the UK, it has been recognised as abuse within the Violence Against Women and Girls strategy. As of July 2019, the Crown Prosecution Service has updated the So-Called Honour-Based Abuse and Forced Marriage guidance to recognize breast ironing as a criminal offence. Notwithstanding these changes, to date there have been no prosecutions. This practice continues in secret and is difficult to detect.

While organisations exist that fight against this act, more still needs to be done.

We need to stop it now and save lives

People need to understand that breast ironing is not capable of solving the larger problems. It is just a branch of a larger tree: gender inequality.

Girls should be seen as equals and taught to respect themselves. Women should understand that sexual abuse is not their fault but the perpetrator's. This way we can wipe away the need for this practice. Sex education for mothers, children, and families should also be integrated into the society.

Lacking restrictions against breast ironing is one of the reasons this practice festers

The law has turned its face away and refuses to protect these girls. No more should we give the excuse of culture when millions are hurting. We have to start prosecuting perpetrators – this will serve as a deterrent and protect victims. Educators need to be alert for signs of breast ironing. Finding out early will be effective in saving girls.

Breast ironing is a global issue that we need to pay attention to. We should work towards affecting solutions and curing these inequalities that devalue women. Most importantly, we have to put an end to sexual violence, as this harmful practice was ignorantly borne as its solution. We have to stop hurting girls and go after perpetrators of this act and sexual abuse.

5 September 2020

This article was first published by girlsglobe.org

The above information is reprinted with kind permission from Girls' Globe

www.girlsglobe.org

Breast ironing: a harmful practice that doesn't get sufficient attention

An article from The Conversation.

By Tamsin Bradley, Professor of International Development Studies, University of Portsmouth

Recent news reports in the UK of breast ironing portray yet more ways in which culture causes harm to young girls. The reports followed renewed calls for stronger action against the practice, which is observed to prevent the development of a girl's breasts and subsequently reduce the sexual attention she may receive. It involves using an object to massage, pound, or press the breasts flat.

Breast ironing is common in West and Central Africa, including Guinea-Bissau, Chad, Togo, Benin, Guinea-Conakry, Côte d'Ivoire, Kenya and Zimbabwe. It's particularly prevalent in Cameroon: there, the number of girls who have been subjected to breast ironing is estimated be as high as one in three (around 1.3 million).

According to the United Nations, 3.8 million teenagers worldwide have been affected by breast flattening. It's estimated that about 1,000 girls from West African communities across the UK have been subjected to the practice, but the figure could be much higher.

While reports on the horrors of female genital mutilation, forced marriage and so-called honour killings are common, people are perhaps less aware of the practice where young girls, as puberty sets in, have their breasts ironed flat.

I have established this during 15 years of research into 'harmful cultural practices' around the world. The practice mirrors ugly misogynistic beliefs and values that underpin other abusive practices. It is ultimately reflective of a power dynamic that demands female submissiveness and complete control over the sexuality of women and girls.

The socialisation of young girls

Breast ironing has been an embedded part of the socialisation of young girls from affected communities for quite some time. The medical consequences can be severe. The practice can include the use of grinding stones, spatulas, brooms and belts to tie or bind the breasts flat. Sometimes leaves which are believed to have medicinal or healing qualities are used, as well as plantain peels, hot stones and electric irons.

The practice is usually carried out by mothers, shamans and healers. Some midwives perform the practice. This makes it a source of income, in a way that's similar to female genital mutilation.

The growth of a girl's breasts during puberty is seen as linked to the emergence of her sexuality; if left unchecked, this will bring 'problematic' and 'destructive' implications for family and community status quo (patriarchy).

However, this gendered reading of the practice is further complicated by research that suggests mothers begin ironing the breasts of their daughters as a way of trying to prevent early marriage and keep daughters in school for longer.

In other words, if a girl's breasts can be held back from developing they will not be viewed as ready for marriage and childbirth and so will be free to continue with their education for longer.

Understanding the drivers behind the practice is obviously critical if routes to change are going to be identified. Clearly breast ironing is not the answer to child marriage. But in contexts where there are few choices, it seems to offer some mothers the only viable way of giving their daughters a little longer to become educated enough to have options.

A global problem

Female genital mutilation and breast ironing needs to be situated within a broader ideology that sees female sexuality as shameful and something to be hidden and denied.

Globally, there are efforts to reverse this mindset. UK Aid, for example, funds a social movement called The Girls Generation which works throughout Africa to reverse the social norms underpinning female genital mutilation.

The replacement of harmful practices such as female genital mutilation and breast ironing with other new rituals that celebrate the female body will hopefully, in time, help reverse these negative views.

Unravelling the prevalence of this practice and the reasons behind it will not be helped by news reporting – as happened in the UK – that depicts breast ironing as evidence of yet more horrors harboured by 'other cultures'.

The focus needs to be on the underlying structural inequalities that continue to devalue the bodies of women and girls. This is a global problem and not something unique to specific parts of the world

2 May 2019

Forced Marriage

What is forced marriage?

Any person may be forced into marriage – this includes people of all ages, genders, ethnicities, and religions.

A forced marriage is where one or both people do not or cannot consent to the marriage and pressure or abuse is used to force them into the marriage. It is also when anything is done to make someone marry before they turn 18, even if there is no pressure or abuse.

Forced marriage is illegal in the UK. It is a form of domestic abuse and a serious abuse of human rights.

Forcing someone to marry isn't always physical, but it is always against the law.

The pressure put on a person to marry can take different forms:

* Physical pressure might take the form of threats or violence (including sexual violence).

* Emotional or psychological pressure might take the form of making someone feel they are bringing shame on their family, making them believe that those close to them may become vulnerable to illness if they don't marry, or denying them freedom or money unless they agree to the marriage.

But when the person who is to get married is aged under 18, doing anything to make them marry is a crime – it doesn't have to be pressure.

In some cases people may be taken abroad without knowing that they are to be married. When they arrive in that country, their passport(s)/travel documents may be taken to try to stop them from returning to the UK.

What is consent?

For a marriage to be consensual, it must be entered into freely by both people getting married. You should feel you have a choice.

Legally, people with certain learning disabilities or severe mental health conditions are not able to consent to marriage, even if they feel the marriage is what they want.

What is an arranged marriage?

When it comes to the marriage of adults, an arranged marriage is not the same as a forced marriage. In an arranged marriage, the families take a leading role in choosing the marriage partner, but both individuals are free to choose whether they want to enter into the marriage.

When it comes to the marriage of children (up to 18), there is no distinction between arranged marriage and forced marriage. Doing anything to cause a child to get married is a forced marriage – and a crime.

> If you consent to marry, but later change your mind – yet still feel that you will be required to go ahead with the marriage – that is a forced marriage too.

What can I do?

If you are in immediate danger call the police on 999.

If you or someone you know is being forced into marriage either in the UK or abroad, you can contact the Forced Marriage Unit.

What is the Forced Marriage Unit?

The Forced Marriage Unit provides support and advice for victims, those at risk, and professionals.

The Forced Marriage Unit can provide advice and assistance both before and after you report to the police, and also if you choose not to report at all. The support offered ranges from providing information and guidance to helping British victims overseas return to the UK.

Caseworkers have experience in dealing with the cultural, social, and emotional issues surrounding forced marriage.

You're not alone

It's not unusual to feel isolated if you or someone you know is being pressured into marriage. But you're not alone. Each year, several hundred cases are reported to us, from women and men of all ages, ethnicities, and religions, including from the LGBTQ+ community. Still, many people do not report what is happening to them, or what they might think is happening to someone they know.

These real-life stories show that forced marriage can happen to anyone, regardless of age, gender, religion, or ethnicity – and that reporting it can save lives. (The names given are not their real names.)

Aisha's story

'I was 15 and just about to finish my GCSEs when I realised that dad was planning to send me abroad to marry my older cousin. Dad was angry all the time and sometimes hit me and my mum. Mum didn't want me to get married so young, but she was too scared to say no to him. I thought dad might trick me into leaving the country and then take my phone off me so I couldn't ask anyone for help.'

Aisha told a teacher at her school, who called the Forced Marriage Unit.

The Forced Marriage Unit worked with children's social care to obtain a Forced Marriage Protection Order, which was served on Aisha's dad. The order prevented the forced marriage from taking place as Aisha's father was unable to take Aisha out of the country and could not apply for a passport on her behalf.

Aisha was scared to stay at home so was given a safe foster placement temporarily. Aisha's mum worked with children's social care and was supported in leaving Aisha's father.

Aisha now lives safely with her mum and younger brothers and was able to finish her GCSEs.

Syed's story

'I was 25 when my parents took me to Pakistan for a family wedding. When I got there I discovered it was me who was getting married. I did not want to but my mum has lots of health problems and everyone said I was making her ill by refusing. After days of saying no I finally gave up and submitted to my family's will. When I got back to the UK, I just tried to forget about it and get on with my life. Then my wife's family started pressuring me to put in a visa application for her to come to the UK. They would call me and threaten me.'

Syed called the Forced Marriage Unit at the earliest opportunity and the Forced Marriage Unit were able to explain how they could assist him as he was a reluctant sponsor.

Khadija's story

'I used to get into trouble at home a lot, for wearing make-up or wanting to stay out late with my friends. My mum didn't like it and we argued a lot. When I was 19, she told me we were going on holiday to visit my grandmother in Somalia. When I got there, my mum dropped me off at a boarding school and told me I had to stay there until I learned to be a good Somali daughter. She took my passport and left me there. The school was really bad. They used to beat us and told me that if I wanted to leave then I had to marry one of the guards.'

Khadija had kept a secret phone hidden. She told her boyfriend what had happened and he called the Forced Marriage Unit.

The Forced Marriage Unit worked with police in the UK to get a Forced Marriage Protection Order, which instructed Khadija's mum to return Khadija's passport, permit her to leave the school, and book her flight back to the UK. The Forced Marriage Unit helped Khadija find short-term safe accommodation when she arrived back in the UK.

She is currently living in a refuge and receiving support from specialist professionals to rebuild her life independent from her family. (The British Embassy Mogadishu does not provide consular services. If you are in Somalia or Somaliland you can contact the British High Commission Nairobi.)

Mandeep's story

'Last night I heard my parents talking about our trip to India this summer and their plan for my brother Mandeep to get married while we are there. My mum said they're getting too old to look after him so thought it would be best for him to have a wife to do so. Mandeep suffers from severe learning disabilities and he is reliant on mum and dad for even the most basic tasks. I really don't think he understands anything about being in a marriage.'

Mandeep's sister contacted the Forced Marriage Unit to highlight her concerns about her brother's situation and his ability to understand what was about to happen to him.

The Forced Marriage Unit made a referral to the local adult social care team explaining the situation and asked if a Mental Capacity Assessment for Mandeep could be completed, ensuring the source of information remained anonymous.

Mandeep was already receiving support from the learning disability team, but they were unaware of the upcoming marriage. Through the assessment, they found that he lacked the capacity to consent to sex and marriage.

Through the advice of the Forced Marriage Unit, a safeguarding plan was put in place, including a Forced Marriage Protection Order. The learning disability team then worked with the family to explain the risk of marriage to Mandeep and explore other options for his long-term needs.

Malcolm's story

'I'm Susan. Malcolm is my dad. He is 75 and over the last five years has become very ill with Alzheimer's disease and his dementia is severe. He cannot remember even the most basic things like where he lives or how to make breakfast. Last summer I was told by his neighbour Pamela that she had booked a holiday for them and they are in love and are planning to get married when they get back. I couldn't believe it. When I asked dad about the situation he couldn't remember saying yes to a trip but thought a holiday might be nice. When I mentioned marriage, he didn't seem to understand.'

Susan wasn't sure this would be defined as a forced marriage so she called the Forced Marriage Unit to ask.

They explained that if Malcolm does not have capacity to consent to marriage, it would be a criminal offence for him to be married.

A capacity assessment was carried out immediately by adult social care. It determined that Malcolm didn't have capacity to consent to marriage and the decision was made for the police to take action to prevent this from happening.

Frequently asked questions

What happens when I call the Forced Marriage Unit?

You will speak to an experienced caseworker who will listen and offer you support and information tailored to your individual circumstances. They will give you information on your rights and the services available to you. We will not contact your family.

Are calls to the Forced Marriage Unit anonymous?

You can remain anonymous if you want but this may limit the amount of support the Forced Marriage Unit is able to provide, so they will often ask for details such as your age, location, and nationality. Any information you share with us will be treated in confidence, unless you are under 18 or there is an imminent risk of harm.

Can you guarantee my safety?

While we cannot guarantee your safety, we can put you in contact with agencies who can help safeguard you. You should always call the police on 999 if you are in immediate danger.

What should I do if I decide to leave home?

Safe accommodation at a refuge may be available to victims of forced marriage and specialist services exist for people from different backgrounds. A refuge is much more than a safe place to sleep. Specialist staff will provide you with the building blocks you need to begin a new life.

What happens if I'm abroad and manage to run away, but I don't have enough money to fly home?

If at all possible, try to take some local currency, a mobile phone with international credit, and a copy of your passport (and if you have residence or immigration documents from another country, take these too). But we can help replace UK travel documents if necessary. Make sure you keep these items safe and hidden.

We can provide advice and help you explore a number of options regarding your return to the UK. A Forced Marriage Protection Order can also be used in certain circumstances to help cover the costs of your repatriation.

How long will it take before I can come back to the UK and where will I stay while arrangements are being made?

We will try to make arrangements for you to come back as soon as possible. However, if you do have to stay abroad for any length of time, we will try to help you find a suitable safe place to stay

If I am abroad, what will happen if I don't have my passport?

Provided you are a British national, we can issue you with an Emergency Travel Document, once we are satisfied of your identity. If you are not a British national, the Forced Marriage Unit would advise you to also contact the nearest Embassy of the country whose nationality you hold to seek help with getting a new travel document.

I got married overseas, is my marriage valid in the UK?

If your marriage is seen as legally valid in the country where it took place, in many cases it will be valid in the UK. You must talk to a solicitor, regardless of whether you had a religious or civil marriage. Religious divorce is not legally valid in the UK.

Can you still help me if I'm under 16?

Yes we can. Please call the helpline to discuss your options.

If I am not a British national can you still help me?

The Forced Marriage Unit can provide support and assistance to anyone in the UK at risk of a forced marriage but we can only provide consular assistance to British nationals (including dual nationals) overseas.

Can I get legal protection to prevent the marriage?

Yes. Forced marriage is a criminal offence in the UK. If you are being forced to marry you can seek legal protection through the civil courts and/or the criminal justice system.

When considering how to protect yourself you can choose whether to take the civil route to seek a Forced Marriage Protection Order, or to go to the police and pursue a prosecution through the criminal court, or both. You can also choose to do neither of these things. The Forced Marriage Unit can help you explore all of the options.

Forced Marriage Protection Orders can be used to prevent someone from being forced into marriage or to protect someone if a forced marriage has already taken place. A person may be arrested if they breach an order. For more information call the Forced Marriage Unit.

'Tip of the iceberg': forced marriage reports soar but true scale of problem still hidden, experts fear

Expert says forced marriage inflicts 'significant damage' and constitutes child abuse.

By Maya Oppenheim, Women's Correspondent

'Devastating' reports of forced marriage to the national helpline have surged as experts warn the issue remains 'rife' but it is difficult to see the true scale of the problem due to people not coming forward.

Exclusive data from Karma Nirvana, which supports forced marriage victims, shows its helpline dealt with 42% more cases between April 2022 and March 2023 than they did in the same period two years before – up from 380 cases in 2020–21 to 536 this year.

This means cases are back to pre-pandemic levels when they handled 533 cases between April 2019 and March 2020.

The figures come as a new study found the number of people coming forward to alert authorities to forced marriage plummeted during the pandemic.

First-of-its-kind research, by the University of Lincoln and the University of Bristol, discovered queries to the government's Forced Marriage Unit sharply declined from 1,507 in 2018 to 337 in 2021.

Experts said the 'alarming' fall was likely to have been caused by COVID-19 rules temporarily curbing forced marriages but added victims, relatives, lawyers, teachers, social workers, and others were also less likely to be able to report forced marriages during lockdowns.

The report, which examined Forced Marriage Protection Orders, issued by the family courts in a bid to stop forced marriages, found around 250 have been approved each year in the past 10 years. This constitutes roughly five orders each week – with researchers warning the issue continues to be 'rife' in England and Wales.

Professor Aisha K. Gill, who co-authored the report, told *The Independent* the 'steady use of' the orders demonstrates forced marriage has not gone away and warned it was not an issue that can be eliminated 'overnight.'

The Professor of Criminology at the University of Bristol argued the pandemic 'exposed and exacerbated pre-existing weaknesses in our public support systems' and 'drove the issue of forced marriage even deeper underground'.

Forced marriage is defined as incidents where one party or both do not agree to the marriage or are not in a position to consent, and it routinely results in rape.

Professor Gill noted 'under-reporting' of forced marriage continues to be a major problem. 'Far from being on the decline, we are just dealing with the tip of the iceberg,' she added.

The academic explained perpetrators are generally parents or relatives and said the practice inflicts 'significant damage' and constitutes not just a 'human rights violation' but also child abuse.

'The coercive element is devastating for these victims,' Professor Gill said. 'We must address this problem and link this with control and abuse and control of sexuality.'

Professor Gill noted the findings demonstrate for the first time how Forced Marriage Protection Orders are a 'double-edged sword' because while they can prevent forced marriage and protect victims, they can also increase the risk of honour-based violence, including abduction, physical assaults, kidnapping, and rape.

There is a 'gendered element' to forced marriage, with the overwhelming majority of cases they looked at involving women victims.

Sundari Anitha, who was also involved in the report, noted Forced Marriage Protection Orders differ from other injunctions for domestic abuse in which the victim will have fled their abuser and the order will bar contact.

The Professor of Gender, Violence, and Work at the University of Lincoln explained most people who seek them continue to live in their family home or remain in touch with the perpetrators, their parents.

She added: 'These young people are trying to balance their need to protect themselves from a forced marriage while avoiding a complete family estrangement.'

The study, conducted in conjunction with the Nuffield Foundation, found the most common age bracket for forced marriage victims was 16 to 21 but sometimes victims were just 11-years-old.

Diana Nammi, executive director of IKWRO, a British charity which helps victims of honour-based abuse, told T*he Independent*: 'Forced marriage is a deep-rooted problem which doesn't disappear from one day to the next. We have dealt with lots of forced marriage cases in the UK since the pandemic.'

Legislation which made it illegal to force someone into marriage in England and Wales was introduced in 2014 and anyone found guilty of doing so can be imprisoned for up to seven years. And a new law banning marriage under the age of 18 came into force in England and Wales earlier in 2023.

25 May 2023

No consent: no choice but to marry their kidnappers

'If a man loves a girl or secretly admires her, he will keep monitoring her movements without her knowledge. One day when she is alone in an isolated place, he will capture her and have sexual intercourse (engagement sex) with her to mark her as his wife.'

– An adolescent girl shared that view with researchers during a focus group discussion in Kidepo-Lobunet Village, Karamoja sub-region in Uganda.

On World Sexual Health Day, which in 2023 had the theme of consent, Communications Officer, Florence Blondel looks at this under-reported type of forced marriage, and what can be done.

'My husband kidnapped me when I was 17. He started beating me three days later. When I was three months pregnant he beat me so hard that I lost the baby.'

– From UNFPA's *Child Marriage in Kyrgyzstan*

In various regions around the globe, spanning Europe, Asia, Africa, and the Americas, young girls and women – especially those below the age of 18 – must fight with their prospective spouses, who are frequently older men.

Scratch that, because it is far worse: they are forcefully seized and captured by their intended partners, often with the assistance of other men, including family members. These vulnerable and overpowered girls consistently find themselves on the losing end of this struggle.

Tragically, in many instances, these girls are completely unaware of the individuals taking them. They are abruptly taken away and oftentimes subjected to sexual assault on the same day.

Their future will all too often be without agency or bodily autonomy – a life of repeated rape.

Marriage by capture: yes, it's still a thing

This is the practice known as marriage by capture. Associated with this is the term 'engagement sex,' or being forced into sexual intercourse with the intent to marry, but it is imperative to accurately label it for what it truly is: rape.

This cruel and repugnant form of forced marriage – known also as bride kidnapping, or marriage by abduction – is defined by coercion, manipulation, and aggression. It is unmistakably rooted in patriarchal norms. This custom instils widespread fear among young girls. It starkly violates human rights and strips these girls of the freedom to chart their own paths, whether it's in seeking quality education, meaningful employment, or choosing life partners.

'In our days, bride capture was a common practice accompanied by the sexual act. Many of those old women you see around were married as a result of bride capture. This practice is still common, especially in village settings. The parents of the boy approach the parents of the girl for negotiations.'

– The role of culture in influencing sexual and reproductive health of pastoral adolescent girls in Karamoja sub-region in Uganda

It is indeed a family affair – but without the victim's knowledge in many cases and rejections are highly discouraged.

Prevalence

This deeply disturbing tradition, which perpetuates gender inequality, is deeply ingrained in certain cultures and accepted. Hard data is not easy to obtain but the countries where it is currently thought to be most prevalent include Ethiopia, Kazakhstan, Kyrgyzstan (where it is referred to as 'ala kachuu' meaning 'to take and run away'), and South Africa.

A 2017 study by researchers at Duke University found that 'between 16 and 23% of women in Kyrgyzstan are abducted for marriage, but the rate is much higher among ethnic Kyrgyz where a third of all marriages are due to kidnapping'.

Amnesty International reports that, according to the Kyrgyzstani Ministry of Interior, 64% of police officers in the southern city of Osh consider 'bride kidnapping' to be 'normal' and 82% of them believe that the abduction is 'provoked' by the women themselves.

In Uganda, there are fears that the appalling practice is increasingly happening across the country. In February, a 17-year-old schoolgirl was taken and 'that very night, the girl victim was sexually assaulted, by the suspect.'

A few months earlier in August 2022, a 14-year-old girl's abduction for marriage was widely shared on social media where a group of eight men grabbed her as her aunt watched. She was whisked off to her expected marital bed where she was 'confined for almost four days'.

The numbers are rising

In a 2022 Internal Labour Organisation (ILO) report, on any given day, roughly 22 million individuals were living in forced marriage in 2021: 'nearly three in every thousand people in the world,' without their consent.

Almost 15 million of them are women and girls. ILO adds that the number keeps rising, with a 6.6 million rise between 2016 and 2021.

'The increase in forced marriage is partially explained by compounding crises including the COVID-19 pandemic, conflicts, and climate change, which have increased the risk of forced and child marriage. These crises have led to unprecedented increases in extreme poverty, lower education rates, a rise in distress migration, and significant increases in reports of gender-based violence. All these factors are associated with increased vulnerability to forced marriage.'

While child marriage is not captured in the ILO figures, it 'is considered a form of forced marriage, given that one and/or both parties cannot express full, free, and informed consent.' Moreover, close to 700 million women and girls living today were married before the age of 18, and 12 million are married off each year according to UNICEF. Some sadly experience the cruellest form of forced marriage – capture.

There should be no justification

'I had to leave the situation or be killed. I know I can never return home because I am considered a dead person for breaking the culture and bringing shame to the families. According to my father, I am dead.'

– Female survivor of three forced marriages

The year is 2023, and yet girls and women remain disrespected and abused through what is supposed to be an archaic, long-forgotten custom. A social norm that should never have existed. Young girls are forced to assume responsibilities beyond their years, including, dealing with sexually transmitted diseases like HIV/AIDS and becoming unwilling mothers, which their bodies are not ready for. According to the Uganda Police Office, it's:

'...a cultural practice that is archaic, unconstitutional and violates the rights of a girl child. The practice puts the girl child at risks of sexual violence on their forced wedding night, draws them into premature motherhood and the pressure to bear children.'

In a paper, *Forced Marriage and Birth Outcomes*, researchers found that 'children born to mothers in kidnap-based marriages have lower birth weight compared with children born to other mothers'.

The number of men, women, and children living in forced marriages has risen globally

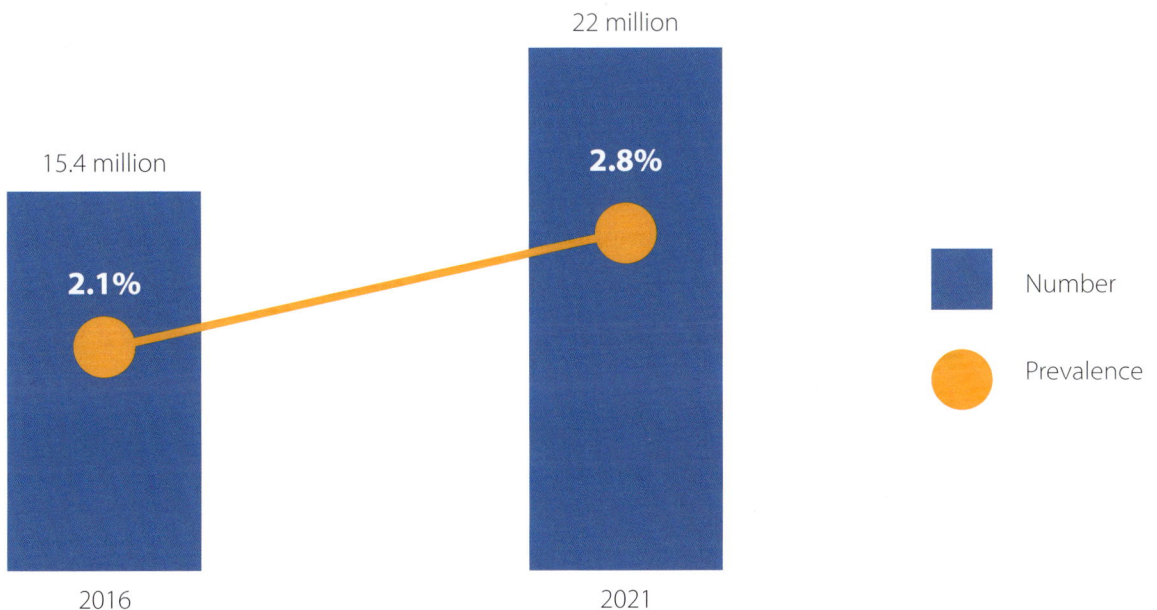

Prevalence (per thousand) and number of people in forced marriage, 2016 and 2021

Note: '%' denotes case per thousand population
Source: Population Matters

The world is **not on track** to achieve gender **equality by 2030**

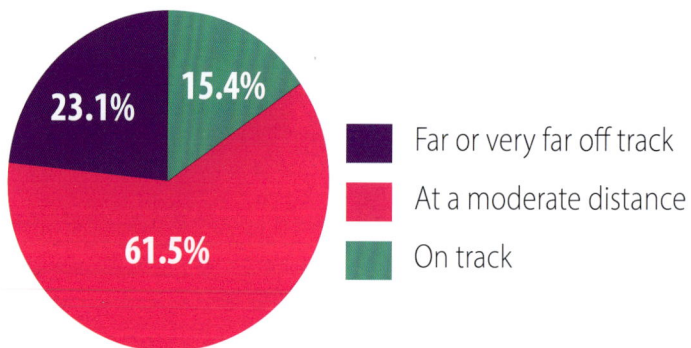

23.1%

15.4%

61.5%

Far or very far off track

At a moderate distance

On track

At the current rate, it will take **300 years to end** child marriage

Nearly half of married women lack decision-making power **over their sexual and reproductive rights**

1 in 5 young women **are married before their 18th birthday**

Source: Population Matters/The Sustainable Development Goals Report 2022

Three in every five people in a forced marriage are in lower-middle income countries

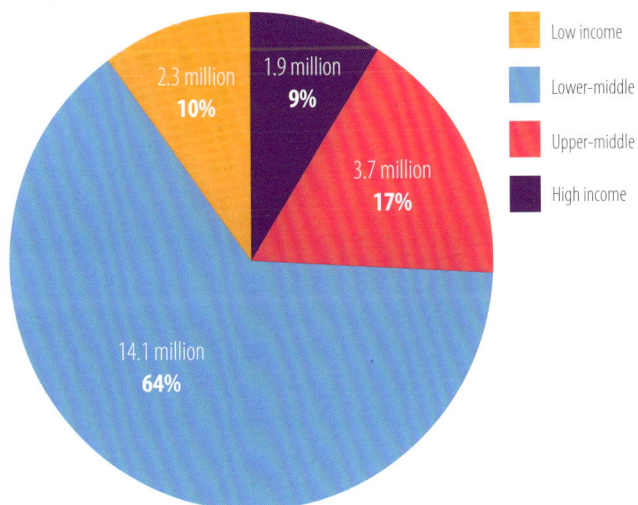

Pie chart legend:
- Low income
- Lower-middle
- Upper-middle
- High income

Chart values:
- 2.3 million — 10% (Low income)
- 1.9 million — 9% (High income)
- 3.7 million — 17% (Upper-middle)
- 14.1 million — 64% (Lower-middle)

Forced marriage by national income grouping: Percentage distribution

Source: Population Matters

'More often, though, having been kidnapped is so shameful that the victim or her family agrees to marriage rather than risk the stigma of being a "used" woman.'

– The above quote is from a Conversation article about bride kidnapping in rural Kyrgyzstan where in 2018 at least two women were killed by their kidnappers when they attempted to resist the marriage.

What to do

Gender inequalities are pervasive and putting us off track for many of the Sustainable Development Goals, including SDG5, which calls for the end of forced marriages.

Ending poverty is vital. While the vile practice of abducting brides has been outlawed almost everywhere, it persists. Some of the reasons it does include poverty.

'Girls and women are forced to marry in exchange for payment to their families, the cancellation of debt, or to settle family disputes.'

In Kyrgyzstan where about one in five Kyrgyz girls is affected by bride kidnapping, they are trying out a mobile game to end the custom since enforcing the law is proving ineffectual.

'The game involves players in the decision-making process and allows them to see from the outside what this or that decision will lead to. Players find allies and receive legal advice, they begin to develop a plan of salvation [for their friend]. Players can get to know their fears, and they can understand that they are not alone and that fear can be fought.'

Education also matters, particularly comprehensive sexuality education. It certainly saved one 15-year-old girl in the Kaabong district, Uganda from this abhorrent yet widely accepted practice, of wrestling girls straight to marital misery.

'If I had not passed through the school, I wouldn't have survived a forced marriage.'

– Joyce Namoe, in World Food Programme video

At Population Matters, we back all these solutions and support women's empowerment projects through our Empower to Plan crowdfunding programme.

Marriage by capture is a pressing issue affecting the lives and dignity of many young girls and women and should be dealt with once and for all.

4 September 2023

The above information is reprinted with kind permission from Population Matters.
© 2024 Population Matters

www.populationmatters.org

How the legal tools to prevent forced marriage can lead to further abuse

An article from The Conversation.

By Sundari Anitha, Professor of Gender, Violence, and Work, University of Lincoln and Aisha K. Gill, Professor of Criminology, Centre for Gender and Violence Research, University of Bristol

Forced marriage – marriage that lacks the consent of one or both parties – is a serious issue which affects 22 million people around the world – predominantly women and girls. In England and Wales, it is a crime that is legally recognised as a form of domestic violence.

In a new report, we paint a full picture of the problem, detailing the experiences of survivors and the challenges in supporting victims of forced marriage.

We interviewed 11 forced marriage survivors and 42 police, domestic abuse and other specialist support providers, analysed 37 court rulings and examined 70 police case files. We found the most common age of women and men subject to forced marriages is 16-21, but girls and boys as young as 11 have also become victims.

Since February 2023, when the minimum age of marriage in England and Wales was raised to 18, any marriage involving a child under the age of 18 also counts as forced.

The majority of victims are women and girls, but people with disabilities and LGBTQ+ people are especially vulnerable. Contrary to popular belief, forced marriages are not limited to specific cultural groups, and have taken place in South Asian, Middle Eastern, Irish, Nigerian and Somali diaspora communities, among others.

The most common method of preventing forced marriages is through a civil injunction called a Forced Marriage Protection Order (FMPO). A potential victim, a relevant third party, such as a friend or lawyer, or any other person with the court's permission (or the court itself) may seek an FMPO.

FMPOs were first introduced in with the Forced Marriage (Civil Protection) Act 2007, which applies to Northern Ireland, England and Wales. Scotland introduced similar laws in 2011.

FMPOs can prohibit perpetrators – usually the victim's parents – from forcing the victim to marry, or taking them overseas for the purpose of marriage. They can also require perpetrators to return the victim to the UK if they have already been taken abroad to marry. Breaching the terms of an FMPO is a criminal offence carrying a maximum five-year sentence.

Approximately 200-250 FMPOs have been granted annually in England and Wales since 2014. We analysed 107 FMPOs issued between 2014-19 to learn more about how they affect victims. Our findings show that the legal tools currently available fall seriously short of protecting victims of forced marriage from further abuse.

Intersecting abuse

While FMPOs are effective in actually stopping a forced marriage from taking place, they do not do much to combat other forms of abuse and violence that take place in the context of forced marriage.

The majority of victims choose to remain in the family home while seeking protection from being forced to marry. In many situations, seeking an FMPO can increase the risk of 'honour-based' violence and other forms of abuse. We found that forced marriage perpetrators commonly resort to emotional pressure, threats, beatings, kidnapping victims abroad, and even torture and rape.

One case we examined in the police files was of a 17-year-old girl of Indian origin. Following her rape, instead of supporting her, her parents blamed her for bringing shame upon them. She was subtly pressured to marry by her father, who told her that she was a burden on their family and marriage was the only way to restore their honour.

She went along with an engagement that she not want to pursue, but subsequently contacted the police. She told them how social services had let her down previously when she reported her rape:

Social services sent me home after keeping me in foster care. […] I am being pressurised to do things I do not want to do like marrying the boy I am engaged to and pressing charges on the boys involved in the [rape] incident last year. […] I have asked for help so many times from my teachers, social workers and police. […] In the past professionals have just gone straight to my parents and told them everything and that just makes things hard for me.

In another case recorded by the police, a 16-year-old girl was taken to Somalia by her parents under the pretext of visiting family. Once there, she was held captive in a detention centre to break down her resistance to a forced marriage. Deprived of her diabetes medication, she regularly lost consciousness.

The same case file detailed the story of another detainee held in the same facility under similar circumstances. She and the 16-year-old girl were rescued at the same time. The other girl described how this 16-year old 'would not wake up even when hit'. Both girls were regularly beaten, burned, had their feet chained, were exposed to extreme weather as punishment, and were tied up without food or blankets and left to defecate on themselves.

In all of these cases, FMPOs helped to prevent a forced marriage and, in the case of the girls held captive in Somalia, helped secure their return to the UK.

Better protection

Many victims struggle to balance their need for protection with the desire to avoid a complete break from their families. They were seeking the protection of FMPOs while living under the same roof as their abuser. Clearly, treating FMPOs as a solution requiring no further action can expose victims to further, serious harm.

FMPOs also have an expiry date – and we found that after they expire, very often the threat of forced marriage resumed. Despite this there are currently no mechanisms for alerting the police to an expiry.

When the police and child or adult protection services work together after an FMPO has been issued, they can create a protective shield that can support victims to make their own decisions about the best way forward. FMPOs are not enough on their own to address the complex and contradictory pressures that victims of forced marriage face. Securing their safety must involve a deeper understanding of coercion and emotional pressure and more long-term support for victims.

7 June 2023

THE CONVERSATION

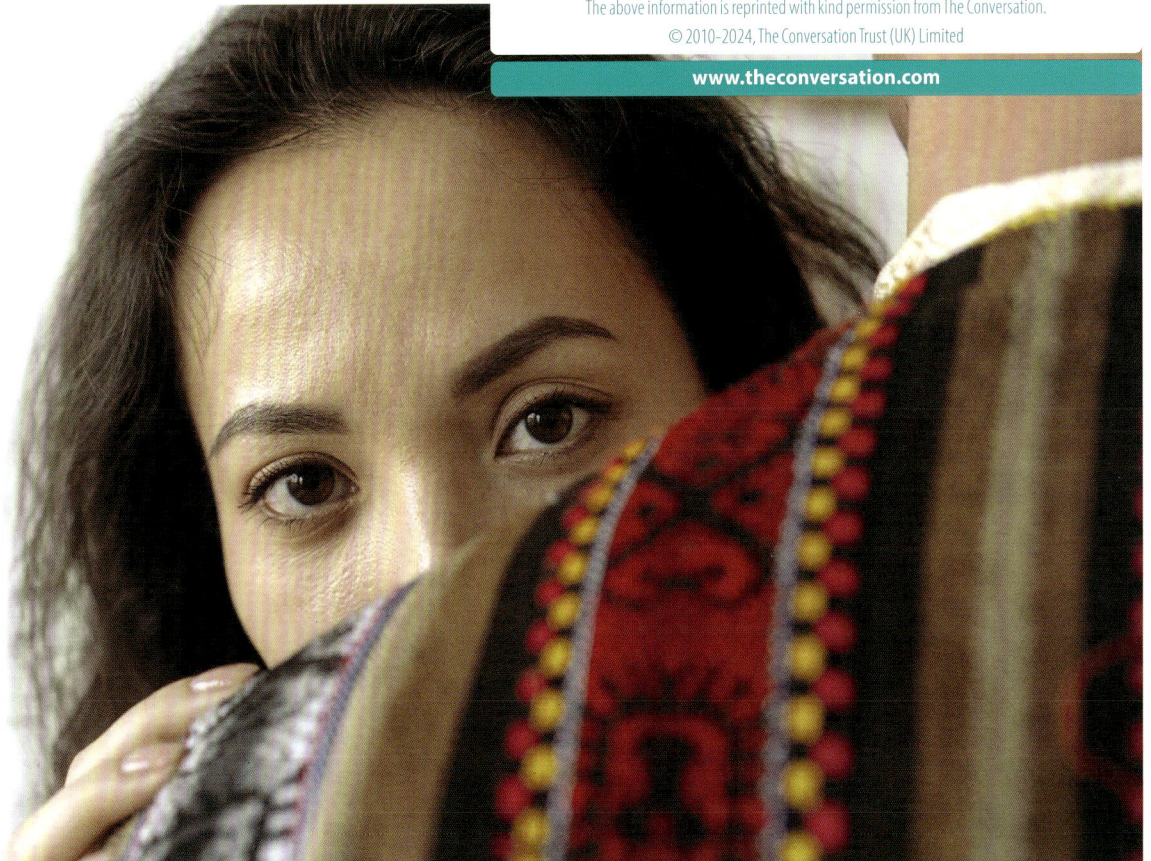

Child marriage

Child marriage and forced marriage

Marriage involving children under 18-years-old is still an accepted practice in many societies. UNICEF estimate that about a fifth of young women worldwide were married before their 18th birthday. Although boys can be affected by the practice, it is mostly girls who suffer slavery as a consequence of child marriage.

Not every marriage involving under-18s will amount to slavery, especially those between couples aged 16 to 18. But in many cases, child marriage causes serious harm to children's physical and psychological health. Increasingly, countries understand the need to protect children from forced marriage.

The 2022 Global Estimates of Modern Slavery show that there has been a significant rise in people living in forced marriages since 2016 – this increase of 6.6 million people includes a significant proportion of children. Overall, 41% of people forced to marry are children, and, while it is very rare for children under the age of 10 to be forced into marriage, the Estimates included reports of children aged 9 who had been forced into marriage.

When is child marriage considered slavery?

Child marriage can be referred to as slavery if one or more of the following elements are present:

- If the child has not genuinely given their free and informed consent to enter the marriage

- If the child is subjected to control and a sense of 'ownership' in the marriage itself – particularly through abuse and threats – and is exploited by being forced to undertake domestic chores within the marital home or labour outside it, and/or engage in non-consensual sexual relations

- If the child cannot realistically leave or end the marriage, potentially leading to a lifetime of slavery.

Children are clearly in a weaker position to give free, full, and informed consent to marriage than adults, even if they appear to 'agree' or don't express refusal.

Many children have little or no control over their movements or person within marriage, including sexual relations. Girls, in particular, are commonly controlled through violence, threats, and humiliation, as well as experiencing isolation and loneliness.

Children may not realistically be able to leave their marriage. For example, they may not be able to support themselves financially or may fear repercussions from in-laws and the wider community, as well as their own families.

Girls who leave their marriages without support are often vulnerable to other forms of slavery and exploitation.

www.antislavery.org

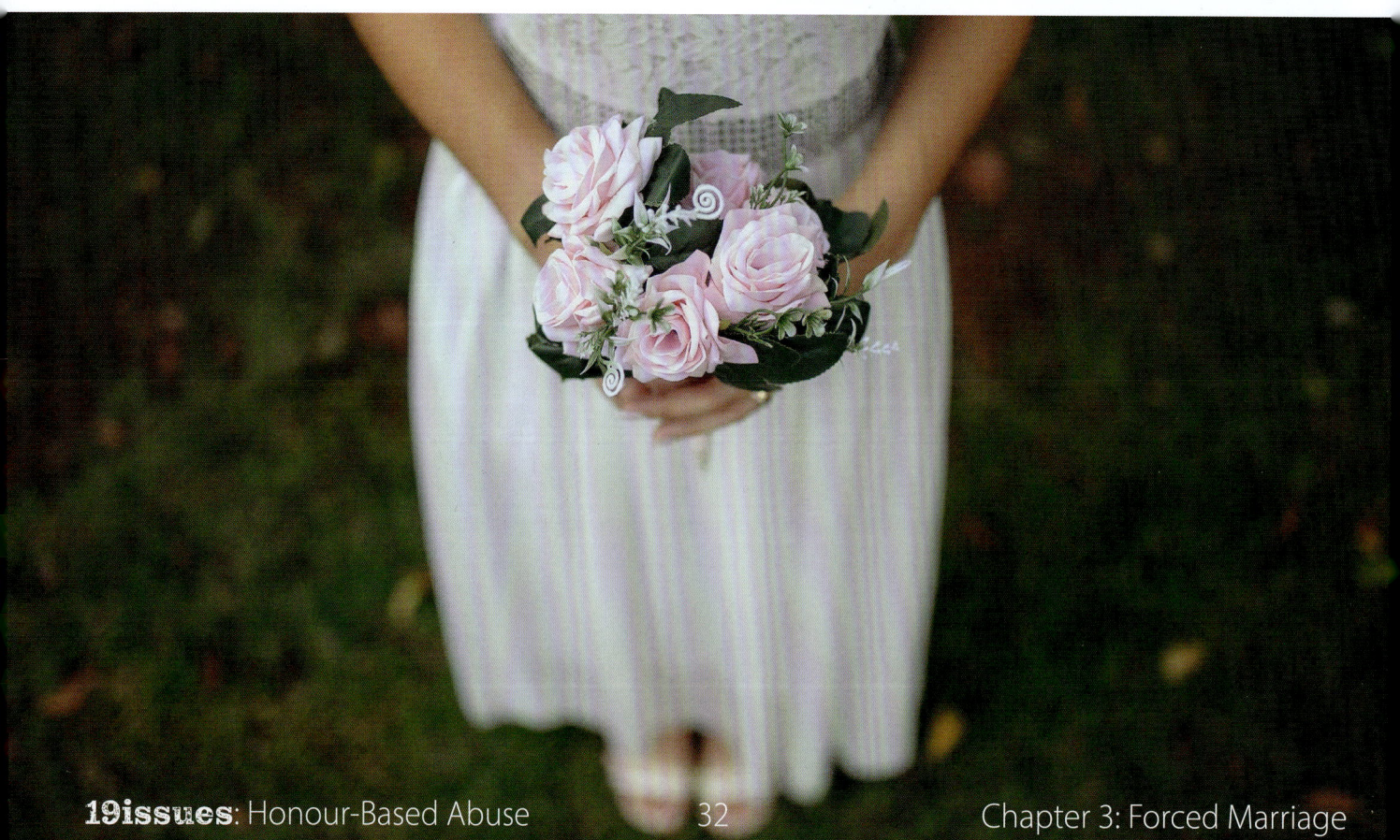

There is no 'honour' in killing or abuse

By The Domestic Abuse Commissioner

Every year in the UK it's estimated that there are at least 12 so-called 'honour killings.'

The victims of these crimes include people like 17-year-old Shafilea Ahmed who was killed by her parents in 2003 for refusing an arranged marriage. She would have been 35 this year.

Honour based abuse is still not understood or widely recognised as an aspect of domestic abuse, but a number of organisations are working hard to tackle the issues and challenge the stereotypes that surround these crimes.

On 14th July, Karma Nirvana, Savera, and the Halo Project all held Day of Memory events to remember victims like Shafilea Ahmed and many others who are subjected to Honour Based abuse and other harmful practices.

Estimates suggest that there is at least one honour-based killing every month in the UK with 7,000 recorded incidents, although many believe that the actual numbers are far higher.

Statistics from Karma Nirvana from 2020/2021 show that 98% of the 1,895 honour based abuse victims that called the helpline were personally connected to the perpetrator and 64% of new callers were suffering honour based abuse from multiple perpetrators.

So-called honour based abuse is motivated by the perceived need to maintain or restore family honour and victims face emotional and often physical abuse for refusing an arranged or forced marriage. It often goes unreported and is often clouded behind the guise of 'culture' or 'tradition.'

Karma Nirvana supports men and women who are victims or survivors of so-called honour-based, and forced marriages. It is working to end honour based abuse.

This year at the seventh annual Day of Memory event, which was set up by Karma Nirvana and *Cosmopolitan* in Shafilea's memory, it launched a new three-year strategy which aims to bring honour based abuse into the mainstream by 2024.

Karma Nirvana wants to encourage statutory and government agencies to respond to honour based abuse as a form of domestic abuse; train frontline workers to understand and respond to honour based abuse; to develop national data to understand the scale of these crimes and to increase the number of specialist safe spaces for survivors and victims.

As the Domestic Abuse Commissioner, I very much support these aims.

A predominant theme running throughout the different events of the Day of Memory is the need for services and individuals to recognise honour based abuse and respond accordingly.

At its event last week Savera – a charity campaigning to eliminate 'honour-based' abuse and other harmful practices, launched its 'One Chance Rule'.

The 'One Chance Rule' recognises that these victims are often very isolated and may only get one chance to speak out which means that it is essential for professionals they come into contact with – like GPs, other health professionals or housing staff, teachers and youth workers – to spot the signs and take action.

Key Facts

- Every year in the UK it's estimated that there are at least 12 so-called 'honour killings.'

- Estimates suggest there is at least one 'honour' killing a month in the UK.

- 14th July is Day of Memory for victims of honour based abuse.

- Once lockdown ended there was a 300% increase in calls to the Halo Project.

Design

Design a poster for the Day of Memory for victims of Honour Based Abuse (14th July).

Domestic abuse is everyone's business and I believe that we all have a role to play to support colleagues, neighbours, friends and family members.

We have seen during COVID-19 that victims of domestic abuse have been increasingly isolated. Many have been trapped with their abuser for months on end. This has been particularly true for those who are subject to honour based abuse.

The Halo Project, which supports victims affected by honour based abuse, forced marriages and female genital mutilation, said in its event that it had seen the impact of victims being cut off.

It saw calls decrease by almost 60% during lockdown but as restrictions eased a 300% increase in referrals and calls.

As a result, it set up a monitored web chat and messaging system to reach those who were isolated by the effects of COVID-19 with fantastic results.

The ways in which these services and so many others are adapting and responding to ensure honour based abuse victims are not forgotten is inspiring, but the Day of Memory for victims like Shafilea Ahmed serve as a stark reminder that there is so much more to be done.

There was no 'honour' in Shafilea's killing or any of the other victims of so-called honour based abuse and we need to work together to eradicate this insidious, invisible form of domestic abuse.

2021

The above information is reprinted with kind permission from Domestic Abuse Commissioner
© 2024 Domestic Abuse Commissioner

www.domesticabusecommissioner.uk

The truth behind honour-based killings

By Sophie Shippe

In 2020, family members murdered two women after a video from the previous year surfaced online of the women kissing a man. This murder is just one of 5,000 'honour-based' killings that happen every year. Girls as young as 15 have died just for helping neighbours elope. Here is some information about honour-based violence.

What is honour-based violence?

Honour killings are one type of honour-based violence. Honour-based violence is any violence that occurs with the purpose of restoring the honour of a family or community, and thus, the victim's family members or community members usually commit it. Violence, in this case, includes any physical or psychological attack. The most common forms of honour-based violence are acid assaults, genital mutilation, forced marriage, and murder. Girls or women typically face the most honour-based violence, but men can be targets as well.

Honour-based violence frequently occurs due to the desire for female purity. The practice stems from cultural ideologies that women belong to men or are a symbol of their family's honour.

Traditionally, some cultures consider men 'guardians of female value,' and therefore, experience dishonour if a woman becomes worthless by destroying her virtue. A woman can experience condemnation for ruining her 'value' even if she suffers rape or assault.

History and statistics of honour-based violence

The practice of honour killings dates back to ancient Babylon, connecting to tribal traditions of burying baby girls alive. Although honour killings have undergone justification in the name of Christianity, Islam, and Sikhism, the practice does not have any basis in religion. On the contrary, religious leaders frequently condemn this violence.

Estimates have determined that about 1,100 people die in honour killings per year in Pakistan. This is only slightly more than in India, which is about 1,000 people. While Pakistan and India record the most honour killings, they are not the only places where these murders happen. Records of honour killings exist in the UK, the US, Sweden, Germany, France, Italy, Turkey, and Uganda. Many places do not document honour killings or record them under other types of violence. Therefore, it is hard to know exactly how many honour killings occur and where they happen.

Activists and artists

While thousands of honour killings happen each year, many activists have been working to change the culture. For one, they are trying to end the legal and colloquial use of the phrase 'honour killing' and instead make sure people use the word murder.

Activists and artists throughout the world have made documentaries about honour killings. In 2016, journalist and activist Sharmeen Obaid-Chinoy won an Oscar for her film *A Girl in the River: The Price of Forgiveness*. The movie follows the story of Saba, a young woman from Pakistan who survived an attempted murder against her after she married without her family's permission.

The film was so influential that the Pakistani Prime Minister vowed to change the laws surrounding honour killings. In fact, that same year, the government passed the Anti-Honour Killing Bill. The bill states that families can no longer pardon people who murder their family members due to 'honour.' Before the enactment of this bill, a family could forgive someone for murdering their family member out of honour. In such a case, the murderer would not receive a charge or penalty.

Obaid-Chinoy is not the only one who has created influential documentaries. In 2021, filmmaker Safyah Usmani worked with MTV and Obaid-Chinoy on her documentary *A Life Too Short*, which follows the life of Pakistani star, Qandeel Baloch, and her death by her brother. While many well-known documentaries have emerged in Pakistan, it is not the only country that features in these films. ITV aired a documentary in 2020 about the murder of a London woman, Banaz Mahmod.

Honour-based violence awareness network

In addition to films, activists have collected resources to help teach people about the tradition. One such project is the Honour-Based Violence Awareness Network that 'intends to advise professionals in how to identify and provide an effective response to these forms of violence, and to provide links to [organisations] with expertise in providing help to people at risk.' Founded by activists Deeyah and Joanne Payton, the website provides training and other informational resources for anyone interested in learning more about honour-based violence.

With films and advocacy groups, awareness about honour-based violence has increased. Increased awareness of the issue, along with an increased pressure to cease such harmful patriarchal practices, will hopefully continue to include policy change.

28 April 2021

Britain's honour crime shame

By Julie Bindel

On Saturday (12 January 2019), Canada granted asylum to Rahaf Mohammed al-Qunun. Detailed in a stream of tweets, the Saudi teenager had refused to board a flight from Bangkok to Kuwait, barricading herself into her hotel room to escape her abusive family. 'My family threatens to kill me for the most trivial things. My life is in danger,' she told journalists.

It is just the latest example of the fear and abuse many women experience in communities in which 'honour-based violence' is the norm. This is nothing short of a disgrace – and the fact that so many police and prosecutors take a 'softly, softly approach' shows us the level of cowardice and incompetence in dealing with this issue.

Originating from tribal customs, primarily in the Middle East and southern Asia, honour crimes can occur in Muslim, Hindu, Sikh, Christian, and Jewish communities. But the victims are mainly girls and women living under Islamic law.

Male family members are required to spy on the female members, with the focus on virginity, chastity and the family's reputation. If the women are seen as violating the 'honour code' by behaving in a way that is forbidden – for example, if she refuses an arranged marriage, is accused of adultery, liaises with a man from another religion, or becomes 'Westernised' – she can be punished for disgracing her family. In countries such as Pakistan or Saudi Arabia, that punishment could be rape or murder.

But honour crime is not restricted to Middle Eastern communities. While the UK may pride itself on being a liberal democracy with one of the finest criminal justice systems in the world, many so-called 'honour crimes' are being committed on British soil – and the UK is tragically failing the women and girls who are the victims.

Across the world, there are an estimated 5,000 honour killings every year, and in the UK, officials estimate that at least a dozen women are victims of honour killings annually, often within Asian and Middle Eastern families.

In 2003 in London, for example, Heshu Yones was murdered by her father for 'becoming too Westernised.' Heshu had run away with her Christian boyfriend but her father tracked her down and cut her throat. In Ireland last year, Thomas Ward was sentenced to 16 months in prison after he punched and kicked his niece as punishment for her escaping an arranged marriage. Ward screamed 'prostitute' and 'whore' as he carried out the attack.

Honour-based violence is the most extreme end of an ideology that says female sexuality should be totally controlled by men. In England and Wales, there were 137,000 women and girls affected by female genital mutilation (FGM) in 2015, and last year the UK's Forced Marriage Unit provided support in well over 1,000 forced marriage cases.

UK police forces recorded 11,744 honour-based crimes between 2010 and 2014, including forced marriage, FGM, sexual and physical assault, and murder. Between 2014 and 2017, the number of incidents reported to the police increased by 53%. And given that honour crimes are often unreported, these figures are likely to underestimate the true scale of abuse. Shockingly, in 2016/2017 just 5% of incidents were referred by the police to the Crown Prosecution Service, the lowest in five years.

In 2015, Her Majesty's Inspectorate of Constabulary had reported that while there are 'pockets of good practice', most police forces need to do more to improve the way they deal with honour-based violence. What on earth is going on here? How can police still be lacklustre in their approach to this so many years after Henshu's death, and with the significant number of training courses available to them?

The first murder in the EU that was recognised as honour-based violence was that of Fadime Sahindal in 2002. She was 26 when her father shot her in the head during a visit to her mother. Fadime, whose family moved to Sweden from a small village in Turkey, had fallen in love with a Swedish man named Patrik. Her father had discovered the relationship and was appalled that she had chosen for herself a man outside of her culture and religion. The case highlights how women from these cultures are treated like chattel; nothing more than goods to be owned and traded.

Fadime's case helped Sweden recognise the dangers women face from communities that impose strict sanctions on them. Fadime was threatened endlessly by her father for four years. Then one day he saw her with Patrik in the street and attacked her, spitting in her face and shouting: 'Bloody whore. I will beat you to pieces.' He murdered his daughter in cold blood. It is mainly because of Fadime that Sweden is the centre of an EU-supported cross-European project on honour crime.

In 2006, the Swedish Liberal politician Nyamko Sabuni popularised the campaign against honour crime when she published her book *The Girls We Betray*. As Integration and Equalities Minister until 2010, Sabuni was responsible for producing the government's first action plan for honour crime.

As well as denouncing what she deemed the 'honour culture' of some immigrant groups, Sabuni proposed banning the veil for girls under the age of 15, compulsory medical examinations to check for FGM, outlawing arranged marriages, and ending state funding of religious schools.

For this, Sabuni has been labelled 'Islamophobic' because she has said migrants should try to adapt to the cultural norms and laws of their adopted countries, and has suggested a ban on religious insignia in schools. 'A lot of people misread their rights,' says Sabuni. 'They think that freedom of religion means that they can do anything in the name of religion, or that human rights means that they can act however they want against others.'

There can be no doubt that Sweden pays less heed to so-called 'cultural sensitivity' than the UK when it comes to dealing with the perpetrators of honour crime. In 2017, the Equalities Minister announced a 10-year national strategy to prevent and combat men's violence against women, including honour-related violence, seeing it not as a 'cultural' issue, but a criminal one.

When I write about religious and cultural oppression of Muslim women, including honour crime, I am routinely accused of inciting 'Islamophobia.' I press ahead regardless, taking my lead from the numerous Muslim-born feminist campaigners that also rail against the niqab, FGM, and forced marriage. Meanwhile, many white liberals, including some politicians and criminal justice agents, shy away.

But change is slowly taking place, thanks to feminists and other human rights campaigners such as Iranian-exile Maryam Namazie, who tirelessly fights against the normalisation of sharia imposed on Muslim-born women in the UK.

However, the UK still lags behind, particularly in respect to FGM, which, even though it was made a criminal offence in 1985, to date, there has not been one conviction, despite an increase in reporting. The UK criminalised forced marriage in 2014, but only after a torturous debate as to whether or not to do so would 'stigmatise' the Muslim community.

Honour crime is committed in any community where women's and girls' lives are deemed worthless, and where laws fail to protect those vulnerable to male dominance and abuse. Any country or community that fails to afford dignity and equality to women should, in my view, be at the very least stigmatised. The word 'honour' has no place in any discussion about rape, murder, and violence, and the perpetrators should bear the brunt of the shame and stigma, not the victims.

14 January 2019

Understanding the story of Banaz Mahmod: a quest for justice and awareness

Banaz Mahmod was born in Iraq in 1985, into a Kurdish family. Seeking refuge, her family moved to the United Kingdom in 1998. However, embedded deep within the cultural practices brought from their homeland, Banaz became ensnared in traditional expectations that ultimately led to her untimely and heartbreaking death.

At the age of 17, Banaz was coerced into an arranged marriage with a man ten years her senior. The marriage, marked by abuse, became unbearable, leading Banaz to return to her family and seek a divorce. Seemingly supportive, her family's attitude drastically changed once she started a relationship with a man she loved – an act her family deemed dishonourable to their name.

Despite reaching out to the police five times, detailing her fears of being killed by her own family, Banaz's pleas were tragically overlooked. In January 2006, her worst fears were realised. Banaz was raped, tortured, and strangled to death. Her body was callously disposed of, hidden away in a suitcase buried beneath a house in Birmingham. It took relentless determination from a specially assigned detective and Banaz's brave boyfriend to bring her murderers to justice, with her father, uncle, and three others finally convicted and sentenced.

Banaz Mahmod's story is heart-wrenching, but it serves as a critical lens through which we examine the intersection of culture, tradition, and individual rights. It brings to light the stark reality of honour killings – a practice where individuals, predominantly women, are murdered by their own families for bringing perceived shame upon their household. These killings, reported globally, reveal a grievous violation of human rights.

A tale of two worlds

Banaz grew up in a community that held tightly to particular cultural traditions, which sometimes clashed with the broader society she lived in. Understanding different cultures and the diversity they bring to our lives is essential. However, it becomes a concern when cultural practices harm individuals, especially when it's against their will.

The heart of the matter

Banaz faced what is known as an 'honour killing' – a tragic, unjust act carried out by her own family. This is a severe and heart-wrenching topic, but it's a reality that needs attention to ensure it doesn't happen to others. Honour killings are acts committed supposedly to protect the reputation or perceived 'honour' of a family or community, but they are, in fact, a grave human rights violation. Banaz's only 'mistake' was wanting to choose her own path in life, including who she wanted to marry – a right that everyone should have.

A struggle for justice

After her disappearance, it took considerable time and effort before justice was pursued. Banaz had reached out to the police for help on five different occasions before her life was tragically cut short. Her pleas for help, sadly, were not taken as seriously as they should have been. This part of her story sheds light on how important it is for authorities to listen and act to protect people's lives, regardless of cultural or social backgrounds.

The ripple effect

Banaz's case had a substantial impact. It prompted a re-evaluation of how the police and other authorities deal with cases of domestic violence and so-called 'honour'-related crimes. Thanks to determined investigators and the unyielding spirit of certain individuals, Banaz's voice was finally heard, even though it was too late for her.

Learning and growing

From the sadness of her story, we can find learning opportunities. Banaz's life encourages us to:

1. **Understand and respect different cultures:** It's important to celebrate diversity and learn about different ways of life. But we should always be critical of cultural practices that are harmful and stand against them.

2. **Value individual rights:** Each person, regardless of their background, has the right to live free from fear and make choices about their own lives without threats or harm.

3. **Understand the role of authorities and trust:** We must work towards a society where everyone, including the police and other services, can be trusted to take every concern seriously and to protect those in need.

4. **Strength in community:** By supporting each other and speaking up against injustices, we become a strong community that looks after all its members.

Reflecting on the issue

While this is a tough subject, especially for young readers, it's a conversation that needs to be held. It's essential to discuss such issues in a safe environment where questions can be asked and knowledge can be gained.

Banaz's story is a tough lesson, but it is through understanding these hard truths that we arm ourselves with the compassion and awareness needed to build a better tomorrow. Every voice counts, and every action, no matter how small, can make a difference. Let's continue to learn, discuss, and take a stand for what's right, ensuring a world where the dignity and choices of every person are respected and protected.

'Her death is not in vain': Bekhal Mahmod says women and girls must be protected from so-called honour based abuse

By Hannana Siddiqui, Head of Policy, Campaigns and Research, Southall Black Sisters

In 2015, 14 July was declared a Day of Memory for victims of so-called honour-based abuse. It marks the birthday of Shafilea Ahmed, who was killed by her parents in a so-called 'honour killing' in 2003. This blog pays tribute to all victim-survivors of so-called honour-based abuse and their bereaved or supportive families and friends.

In her newly released memoir, *No Safe Place*, Bekhal Mahmod recalls a history of repeated abuse from her parents, particularly her father, for being a 'troublemaker' – a rebellious child who refused to accept her botched female genital mutilation (FGM) and other restrictions on her body and mind in order to control her sexuality as a girl and then as a young woman. She was first beaten when she was only six for innocently touching her much older male cousin's odd-looking fingernails, leaving her confused and frightened of her own parents.

'There were no explanations about why I was being beaten until after the beating. No one tells you what is right and wrong. I had to learn the hard way. And even then, I could not agree with my parents about what was right and wrong. I thought their so-called 'honour' was just 'dishonour' and 'disloyalty.' 'How can you betray your own children by killing and abusing them?' Bekhal said.

The FGM, which nearly killed Bekhal, was a turning point for her. Even at the age of eight, Bekhal realised that FGM was wrong and that she did not want the traditional life. Her culture and religion required that she was forced to wear a hijab against her wishes, and that she was restricted to the home and to early marriage.

She wanted freedom and saw the possibility of escape when the family moved to the UK as asylum seekers. She faced both racism at school and abuse at home. However, Bekhal had been inspired by 'girl power' and women's rights organisations to become even more defiant. Her parents sought to control her by planning a forced marriage to her much older cousin and sending her back to Iraqi Kurdistan when she was only 15. Bekhal knew that in order to survive, she had to leave the very people she loved. She left home three times. She returned the first time due to threats to her life from her father.

The second time, Bekhal was placed in foster care, but returned home again after the social worker passed on a tape recording from her parents where her father threatened to kill the whole family. Her brother also attempted to kill her on the instructions of his father.

Bekhal's departure also led to the child marriages of her younger sisters, Banaz and Payzee, and later, the murder of Banaz, creating deep feelings of regret and guilt in Bekhal.

Bekhal said: 'I had left home, and because of this "shame," my sisters were forced into marriage to save the honour or reputation of the family. Banaz later complained to the police that her husband raped and beat her. He treated her like his 'shoe,' which is what she told me when I last secretly saw her in 2005. I begged her to come with me – but she loved my mother and did not want to bring the family shame. How I wish I had taken her with me. For soon after this meeting, Banaz, who finally decided to leave her husband and fell in love with another man, her "prince," but of whom the family system. However, despite having achieved justice, Bekhal had to enter a witness protection scheme for her own safety and will be in hiding for life.

'Although I have lost my family and old friends, and miss my younger sisters, I still think that it is right I gave evidence against my father and uncle. How could I have lived with myself if I hadn't? Banaz deserves justice. All victims deserve justice,' Bekhal reflects.

Banaz's killers were hailed as heroes by their community in the UK and Iraq. The uncle claimed that he felt no shame as he had 'done justice.' Although he and most of the others denied the murder at court, implicitly they were attempting to influence the judge and jury by justifying the so-called 'honour killing' as legitimate within their culture and religion.

'Although my father and uncle received minimum prison sentences for 20 and 23 years respectively, I do not think this is long enough. Banaz could have lived for much longer and had a family of her own which she most desired, had they not murdered her; and I am sentenced for life to grief, fear and loneliness. Their sentences should reflect this pain and loss.'

Bekhal is calling for 'The police need regular training on honour based abuse; and groups like Southall Black Sisters need proper funding to help victims and to empower women in minority communities.'

14 July 2022

did not approve, was murdered in cold blood to restore their precious so-called family 'honour."

Banaz was raped and strangled on 24 January 2006. Her father, uncle (a powerful community leader who instigated the crime) and five male cousins conspired in a 'council of war' to kill her and her boyfriend. The couple had reported threats and attempts to kill to the police. In total, Banaz had gone to the police five times, and even named the suspects who later went on to kill her. It appears that the police did not intervene out of 'cultural or religious sensitivity.' Later, a police complaints watchdog found serious failings in the police's handling of the case.

'My sister, who had turned to the police for protection, was instead turned away five times, even when her own father tried to kill her in 2005. The police officers with the most serious failing only received 'words of advice' – that is like slapping their wrists when they should have been sacked. How can the police give confidence to women in coming forward to seek help when officers are not disciplined and the system improved?'

Although the investigating officers before Banaz's death had failed her, those who investigated her death had gone beyond and above to bring the case to justice. Bekhal was the first daughter in history to give evidence at the Old Bailey in 2007 leading to the convictions of her father and uncle for murder. The other five men were also prosecuted and found guilty or admitted guilt to murder or related crimes. Two had to be extradited from Iraq to where they had fled after the murder- another first for the British legal

www.domesticabusecommissioner.uk

Where Can I Find Help?

Below are some telephone numbers, email addresses and websites of agencies or charities that can offer support or advice if you, or someone you know, needs it.

24hr Domestic Violence Helpline

(run in partnership between Refuge and Women's Aid)

Freephone: 0808 2000 247 (24 hours)

www.nationaldomesticviolencehelpline.org.uk

Ashiana Network

www.ashiana.org.uk

FCO Forced Marriage Unit

Helpline: 020 7008 0151 (or 0044 20 7008 0151 if you are overseas)

Muslim Women's Network Helpline

Tel: 0800 999 5786

Text: 07415 206 936

Email: info@ mwnhelpline.co.uk

www.mwnhelpline.co.uk

Halo Project Charity

Tel: 01642 683 045

Email: info@haloproject.org.uk

www.haloproject.org.uk

Southall Black Sisters

Helpline: 0208 571 0800

www.southallblacksisters.org.uk

Honour Network - Karma Nirvana

Helpline: 0800 5999 247

www.karmanirvana.org.uk

Iranian & Kurdish Women's Rights Organisation

Helpline: 0207 920 6460 (Mon–Fri, 9.30-5.30)

24/7 Emergency numbers:

Kurdish/Arabic 07846 275246

Farsi/Dari/Turkish 07846 310157

www.ikwro.org.uk

Hemat Gryffe Women's Aid Glasgow

Helpline: 0141 353 0859

www.hematgryffe.org.uk

Freedom Charity

Helpline: 0845 607 0133

Alternatively you can text us for help, text the words 4freedom: to 88802

NSPCC

www.nspcc.org.uk

Childline

Helpline: 0800 1111

www.childline.org.uk

Against Forced Marriages by JAN Trust

Helpline: 0800 141 2994

www.againstforcedmarriages.org

Savera UK

Helpline: 0800 107 0726 (Mon– Fri, 10am–4pm excluding Bank Holidays)

www.saverauk.co.uk

The Dahlia Project

Tel: 0207 281 9478

Email: dahlia@manorgardenscentre.org

www.dahliaproject.org

FORWARD

Tel: 0208 960 4000

Email: support@forwarduk.org.uk

www.forwarduk.org.uk

If you need help, you can contact any of the organisations/charities above, or you can speak to a trusted adult such as a teacher or your GP.

If you are in immediate danger call 999.

Further Reading/ Useful Websites

Useful websites

www.antislavery.org

www.borgenproject.org

www.domesticabusecommissioner.uk

www.girlsglobe.org

www.gov.uk

www.independent.co.uk

www.karmanirvana.org.uk

www.parliament.uk

www.populationmatters.org

www.respect.org.uk

www.safeguardinghub.co.uk

www.theconversation.com

www.theguardian.com

www.unherd.com

www.victimsupport.org.uk

Further reading*

Killing Honour by Bali Rai

No Safe Place: Murdered by Our Father by Bekhal Mahmod

Cut: One Woman's Fight Against FGM in Britain Today by Hibo Wardere

Overcoming: My Fight Against FGM by Dr Ann-Marie Wilson

Tell Me Your Story: Maasai Girls on Surviving FGM and their Hopes for the Future by Christabel Ligami

Saving Safa: Rescuing a Little Girl from FGM by Waris Dirie

Disgraced: Forced to Marry a Stranger, Betrayed by My Own Family, Sold My Body to Survive, This is My Story by Saira Ahmed & Andrew Crofts

Shame: The bestselling true story of a girl's struggle to survive by Jasvinder Sanghera

Forced to Marry Him: A Lifetime of Tradition and the Will to Break It by Davinder Kaur

But It's Not Fair by Aneeta Prem

* Please note that due to the subject matter, some of these books may not be suitable for younger readers. Please see your librarian for advice.

Pages 26–29: Child Marriage in Kyrgyzstan, https://eeca.unfpa.org/sites/default/files/pub-pdf/unfpa%20kyrgyzstan%20overview.pdf

World humanitarian day: 'WFP school meals save many girls from forced marriages', https://www.wfp.org/stories/world-humanitarian-day-wfp-school-meals-save-many-girls-forced-marriages

Glossary

Breast flattening/ironing

A process whereby young girls' breasts are flattened, ironed, massaged, and/or pounded down to delay the appearance or development of breasts entirely.

Child marriage

A child marriage refers to anyone under the age of 18 in any formal marriage or informal union with an adult or another child. It is a violation of human rights, and is a form of forced marriage.

Coercive control

The term coercive control refers to the aspects of domestic violence that encompass more than just physical abuse, e.g. psychological behaviour that removes a victim's freedom.

Domestic abuse

Any incident of physical, sexual, emotional or financial abuse that takes place within an intimate partner relationship. Domestic abuse can be perpetrated by a spouse, partner or other family member and occurs regardless of gender, sex, race, class or religion.

Female Genital Mutilation Act 2003

A UK law making it an offense for any person in England, Wales or Northern Ireland to perform FGM or to assist a girl to carry out FGM on herself. It is also an offence to assist a non-UK national or resident to carry out FGM outside the UK on a UK national or permanent UK resident.

Female genital mutilation (FGM)

Female genital mutilation is a non-medical cultural practice that involves partially or totally removing a girl or woman's external genitalia. The procedure is harmful, with both physical and psychological effects. It is a form of child abuse, and violence against women and girls.

FGM tourism

The process of taking a girl abroad in order to have FGM performed. A criminal offence under the Female Genital Mutilation Act 2003

Forced marriage

A marriage that takes place without the consent of one or both parties. Forced marriage is not the same as arranged marriage, which is organised by family or friends but which both parties freely enter into.

Forced Marriage (Civil Protection) Act 2007

A law established to safeguard individuals from being coerced into marriage against their free and full consent, and to protect those who have been forced to enter into marriage without such consent.

Forced Marriage Protection Order (FMPO)

A court protection order that protects a person from any attempt to be forced into marriage, or for those already in a forced marriage.

Forced Marriage Unit

Run by the Home Office and Foreign, Commonwealth and Development Office in the UK to provide advice and support to victims and potential victims of forced marriage.

Honour-based abuse (HBA)

So-called honour-based abuse (HBA) and honour-based violence (HBV) are crimes or incidents committed in order to protect or defend the 'honour' of a family or community. It can include practices such as forced marriage, emotional, psychological, sexual, and physical abuse, and even murder, and is a violation of human rights.

Honour crime/killings

An 'honour' crime or killing occurs when family members take action against a relative who is thought to have brought shame on the family. The victims are mostly women who are accused of dishonouring their family by going against their wishes (for example, by fleeing a forced marriage).

Marriage by capture

Also known as bride kidnapping, marriage by abduction, and engagement sex, it is a practice whereby a man abducts the woman he wants to marry. Historically documented in many cultures around the world, it is widely condemned as a violation of human rights, and is now illegal in many countries. It is not a lawful marriage, and as is considered a form of violence against women.

Slavery

A slave is someone who is denied their freedom, forced to work without pay, and considered to be literally someone else's property. Although slavery is officially banned internationally, there are an estimated 27 million slaves worldwide. Article 4 of the Universal Declaration of Human Rights states that 'No one shall be held in slavery or servitude; slavery and the slave trade shall be prohibited in all their forms'.

Virginity testing

This is an examination of the female genitalia in order to establish whether the girl or woman has had vaginal sexual intercourse. Described by the World Health Organisation (WHO) as a 'harmful practice' with 'no scientific merit or clinical indication', there is no known examination that can prove whether a woman has had vaginal intercourse.

Index

A
action, taking
    forced marriage 30
    harmful practices 11–12, 20, 21
    honour-based crimes 34, 35, 39–40
    reluctance 8, 12, 20
    risks 31–32
Ahmed, Shafilea 34
arranged marriage 23

B
breast ironing 20–22
British Somalis 14–15

C
child marriage 28, 33
communities affected 1, 3–4, 5, 36
Covid-19 lockdowns 8, 26, 34
cultural sensitivities 8, 20, 37

D
data collection 3–4
definitions, official 1, 3, 8

E
education 4, 22, 30

F
family courts 9
FGM (female genital mutilation)
    effects on health 11, 13
    experience of 18–19
    prevalence 10
    prosecution for 16
    safeguarding 14–15, 16–17
    types 10
forced marriage
    child marriage 33
    experiences of 24–25
    marriage by capture 27–30
    prevalence 9, 26, 27–28
    support for victims 23–24, 25, 31–32
Forced Marriage Unit 23–25

G
gender inequality 21, 29

H
health
    breast ironing 20
    FGM 11, 13
help, getting 2, 11, 23, 25
honour-based crimes 3–4, 9, 34–40

K
Karma Nirvana 5–6, 34
kidnap (marriage by capture) 27–30
killing, honour-based (murder) 35,
    36–37, 38, 40

L
laws
    breast ironing 20, 21
    FGM 11, 13, 16–17
    forced marriage 26, 31
    honour-based abuse 8
LGBTQ+ 6, 18–19

M
Mahmod, Banaz and Bekhal 38–40
male victims 5–6
marriage by capture 27–30

P
perpetrators 1, 3
police
    recording 3, 7, 9
    response 6, 16, 38, 39–40
poverty 30

R
racism 14–15
rape 27–28
reasons
    harmful practices 11, 20, 21
    violence 2, 35
refugees 18–19
religion 1, 3, 11, 35, 37
reporting, barriers to 3, 4, 7–8

S
schools and FGM safeguarding 14–15,
    16–17
sexuality 6, 22
slavery 33
support for victims 6, 23–24, 25, 31–32,
    34

T
types of honour-based abuse 2, 3–4